Coutts Lindsay

Coutts Lindsay

1824 – 1913

VIRGINIA SURTEES

MICHAEL RUSSELL

© Virginia Surtees 1993

First published in Great Britain 1993
by Michael Russell (Publishing) Ltd
Wilby Hall, Wilby, Norwich NR16 2JP

Typeset by The Spartan Press Ltd
Lymington, Hampshire
Printed and bound in Great Britain
by Biddles Ltd, Guildford and King's Lynn

Indexed by the author

Contents

CONTENTS

List of Illustrations

LIST OF ILLUSTRATIONS

Acknowledgements

It is to the Earl of Crawford and Balcarres that I owe this book. Without exacting any conditions he has allowed me to make full use of his family correspondence deposited at the National Library of Scotland, as well as placing further papers at my disposal, while willingly and patiently replying to innumerable questions. My debt of gratitude is a large one and this embraces the kindness I have had from Lord and Lady Crawford at Balcarres.

The depth of my obligation to Mr Nicolas Barker is of another kind. His history of the *Bibliotheca Lindesiana* which as a source book has guided me through the labyrinths of the Crawford, Balcarres, and Lindsay families, has been invaluable as has also his stimulating observations and the help which he has afforded me.

Mr Leopold de Rothschild's liberality in allowing me access to the Rothschild Archive and thus making available a component part of this book has been a contribution of great value for which I thank him.

From Mr Fredric Wilson, Curator, Pierpont Morgan Library, I have had so generous a response that I am once again in the debt of that great Library.

Over many months I have been the recipient of help and tolerance from the staff of the National Library of Scotland, and in particular from Miss Jean Cromarty. I take this opportunity of renewing my thanks to her, as I do likewise to Miss Simone Mace, archivist to the Rothschild Archive who, with her assistant, Miss Julia Harvey, has been tireless in searching for relevant material by which I have benefited immeasurably.

ACKNOWLEDGEMENTS

For very particular help I am grateful to Miss Elizabeth and Miss Mary Brameld; the Hon. Mrs Brudenell; Lady Aline Cholmondely; Mr John Christian; Mr John Gere, Secretary of the Dilettanti Society, and to its Librarian, Mr Bernard Nurse; Dr David Hay; Mr James Hervey-Bathurst; Professor Arthur Jacobs; Mr Richard Jefferies, Curator of the Watts Gallery; Mr John Lindsay Jopling; Miss Bridget Keane, Brent archives; Mr J. G. Links; Mr Barry Lock; the London Electricity Board; Dr Rosalind K. Marshall, Scottish National Portrait Gallery; Mr Michael Meredith; Dr Olwen Niessen; Mr Terence Pepper, National Portrait Gallery archives; Mr Nicholas Savage, Royal Academy Library.

In various ways I have also been assisted by Mr Paul Atterbury; Mr Gordon Baldwin, J. Paul Getty Photograph Library, Santa Monica; Miss Judith Bronkhurst; Major R. M. Collins; Mrs John Gere; Miss Lis Hissink; Mr Alyn Giles Jones; Miss McComish, National Gallery archives; Mr Jeremy Maas; Miss Glenise Matheson; Mr J. P. Pearce, Coutts & Co. archives; Mr John Surtees.

To the following institutions I owe thanks for allowing me to quote from material in their possession: the Beinecke Rare Book and Manuscript Library, Yale University; the British Library; Castle Howard archives; Cornell University; the Huntingdon Library, San Marino; Oxford University Press; the Pierpoint Morgan Library, New York.

Where no source reference is given information is from the family papers of Lord Crawford. Spelling has not been adjusted and points of omission have not been introduced.

I

The Lindsays

When George Richmond reached Rome with his wife and son in 1837 to further his art studies, he was resolved that with hard work and application he would master the skills of portrait painting and thus make for himself the position he came eventually to hold at home. He had buried three sons in England; this was the time to come abroad. A happy occurrence was the commission given by Lord Lindsay, who was joining with his cousins and their children in the enjoyment of a gentler climate while gratifying a passion for leisured sightseeing and scholarship.

Alexander Lord Lindsay, the eldest son of the 24th Earl of Crawford and 7th Earl of Balcarres,[1] who would succeed as the 25th Earl of Crawford, had come to Italy to join his first cousin once removed, Colonel James Lindsay, and his wife Anne. He cared for these two perhaps as much as for his own parents, and it was of their four children, to whom he showed a like affection, that in 1839 Richmond executed his commission in watercolours.

The distant sunlit landscape of the Roman *campagna* forms an idyllic backdrop to this conversation piece, while the eye focuses immediately, not on the little boy still in skirts feeding a goat, nor on his two sisters, but on the older brother on a folding stool. He is fifteen years old but in appearance almost a young man.

This is Sir Coutts Lindsay, baronet at thirteen, the golden boy, the legendary figure of later years, a talented painter and loving son, fatally attractive to women and a faithless husband. Already the artist, he is making a drawing and sits in profile, presenting the neat well-defined features reflected in Julia Cameron's familiar portrait-photograph taken some thirty years later. His hair is thick and curls, his white, wide-collared shirt is Byronic in appearance and romantic in effect.

Coutts – the name is of Celtic origin – was born on 2 February 1824 at Brandsbury (now Brondesbury), the country house of his maternal grandfather, Sir Coutts Trotter, Bt. This was a pleasant estate of sixty acres beyond the Kilburn turnpike extending towards Edgware, and except for one journey north it was to be the limit of the child's horizon in his early years.

In the last quarter of the eighteenth century Brondesbury had been acquired by Sarah Lady Salusbury, second wife and now widow of Sir Thomas Salusbury, a judge of the Admiralty Court, but, of greater interest to Johnsonian admirers, the paternal uncle and sometime benefactor of Hester Thrale Piozzi. Displaying good judgement in her wish to improve her property, Lady Salusbury had consulted Humphry Repton, the landscape gardener, in early 1789 and within two months had been presented with the first of his Red Books.[2] A few simple proposals to which she agreed were designs for new plantations in a landscaped park and the addition of a haha. The house, which he did not touch, stood on a slightly elevated piece of ground. Built in the mid-eighteenth century it was of no particular architectural merit but was pleasantly solid and of a commodious size. The roof was surmounted by a small cupola supported by arches; later a bay-window was thrown out on the garden side. An entrance lodge, carriage drive, a sheet of ornamental water, conservatory, orchard, stables, a laundry, a large paved dairy and poultry houses completed the estate. Looking back with a childhood's recollection, it had seemed as if the sun never shone anywhere so brightly, nor hay ever smelt so sweet or grass looked so green.

Sir Coutts Trotter, owner of the property since 1807, was a man of discrimination and taste. Said to have 'a fine aristocratic countenance', he was very tall and reserved in manner. Named after his godfather, Thomas Coutts, the founder of the banking firm, he had entered the partnership in 1793, was created a baronet in 1821 and senior partner five years later. Having been left a childless widower he remarried, and in 1802 Anne, the elder of two daughters, was born. There were no boys, the baronetcy passing by special remainder after his death to Coutts, his eldest grandson.

Anne Trotter was of no common clay. From her father she had inherited something of his stature; her finely modelled features and unaffected bearing marked a strikingly handsome appearance. But more than this, her warm, sociable nature was nicely balanced by a sound knowledge of European literature and history and a deep appreciation of art. She was just twenty when she married a colonel in the Guards eleven years her senior.

James Lindsay, for this was her husband, combined an impressive appearance with absolute integrity; he had served at Walcheren and in the Peninsular Wars and was regarded with respect. A good amateur artist, he possessed a happy disposition and drew strength from a steadfast faith. The Lindsays, in a long and distinguished descent, had been established in Scotland by the twelfth century, since when the family could count statesmen, ambassadors to England (notably to King John), a Chancellor of Scotland, book-collectors and soldiers among its ranks. An earldom was granted in 1398; the father of the 6th Earl of Crawford had fallen at Flodden Field; the 16th Earl had fought at Marston Moor. Chivalry, scacrifice and loyalty were the foundation of their house. Nearer to our time, Lady Anne Barnard, sister of the 6th Earl of Balcarres, now best known as the author of the ballad 'Auld Robin Gray', was famous in her day for her brilliance of speech and wit. While still young

she had been able to hold her own in conversation with Dr
Johnson and by her enduring interest in her family's past
history and her enthusiasm in collecting their papers and
reminiscences she had won the lasting admiration of Sir
Walter Scott. In 1784 she had accompanied Mrs Fitzherbert
abroad in her flight from the Prince of Wales's over-
demonstrative affection and had earned the confidence of
both.

It was her nephew, this same James Lindsay, soon to
inherit Balcarres in Fife, the home of the family since the end
of the sixteeth century, who in 1822 would take his bride,
Anne Trotter, to a posting in Dublin with the Grenadier
Guards; there he was soon promoted to lieutenant-colonel.
Anne Lindsay returned to Brondesbury for the birth of their
first child in 1824. Three more followed after Coutts:
Margaret (Minnie), born at the very end of the same year,
Mary (May), and Robert (Bob), ten years younger than his
brother, whose future distinction was the award of the first
Victoria Cross, won in the Crimea.

2

Sir Coutts Lindsay, Bt

From birth Coutts was the darling of those around him at Brondesbury where he spent his first years. At seven months Sir Coutts Trotter was noting his weight (one stone and five pounds) while his paternal grandfather had never been known to manifest such tenderness as he did for the child. His mother's admiration was boundless. 'Couttsy, the darling, is lovely,' she wrote to the boy's father, 'his cheeks burning with roses and his eyes and dimples laughing in archness and merriment.' She could hardly imagine anything more engaging than he was at three years. 'His eyes beam with sensibility and sparkle with animation and everything he does is full of energy and intelligence.' The reports were sometimes at variance, for though 'lively to a curious degree, he is such a frail looking little flower – so like a sprite. As docile as a lamb with the spirit of an Arab horse, though the spirit sometimes wears out the delicate little frame.' She thought his intelligence increased every day; he could repeat three verses of the 'Busy Bee' without prompting. By the time he was four he was bright enough to appreciate his sovereignty. 'Grandpapa says Coutts is captain,' he told his nurse. According to a sister of Sir Coutts Trotter, the 'Captain' at four years old was so busy running on the lawn with a dead jackdaw, his flaxen curls blowing in the air and the urgency of his face blooming and beautiful, that from morning till night he could ill spare a moment for the society of the grown-ups.

He was caught petitioning the cook 'in the smoothest manner to send up a tart for his dinner and a little "small beer". He is assuredly a noble boy.' The fatal charm was already at work. An endearing vignette remains of Coutts at Balcarres taking leave of Hay, his grandfather's faithful old servant. Coutts had been given a trifling present to give Hay who could not bring himself to look at him for tears. 'Hay, take this from Couttsy,' said the child, who far from making a commonplace bow, turned to make Hay the most elegant curtsy.

At six, in his desire to impress where he knew he was cherished, he let the truth fall victim to his imagination. Out in the fields one day a hare was started. Off flew Coutts after it, cleared a dyke at a bound and never stopped till the hare fairly outdistanced him. On his return 'his dear little rosy cheeks and sparkling eyes spoke volumes for the happiness he had enjoyed', and so enchanted was he with his pursuit that he told six lies without stopping, amongst others that he had killed the hare with a stick he carried; also that he had broken its leg.

Letters between Brondesbury and Dublin were not entirely on the subject of Coutts. Anne could write of her other children, also of her father's failing health. He was given to odd little turns of mind such as when one child was ill and would have liked some grapes, Sir Coutts preferred their shrivelling untouched in the hot-house so that he might see them hanging. For social news there was a party where Anne met General and Mrs FitzRoy ('this last oldish and rather disagreeable') and Mrs Nathan Mayer Rothschild with two sons and a daughter, Charlotte, the young bride of her first cousin Anselm Salomon von Rothschild. Had Anne a crystal ball she might have seen that thirty-eight years later her adored Coutts would marry a FitzRoy yet unborn whose mother, Hannah, was the sister of this same Charlotte of 1826.

James Lindsay, still in Dublin with his regiment, had no cause for crystal gazing. On the contrary, his mind was on more practical levels, worrying that Coutts was in-sufficiently clad in winter. He recommended flannels and worsted stockings. 'Worsted stockings are indispensable to happiness during the winter.' Coutts was immediately put into trousers worn with a cloth pelisse and a little beaver hat.

But by 1832 Coutts's sunlit days were coming to an end. Indications, not wholly favourable, marked him as a variously imperfect child. Perhaps too much admiration had been lavished on him for his own good. Goals had been too easily won; there had been no adversary to usurp his role of 'captaincy'. Adored as he was by his sisters, and himself a most loving child, the family was united by the tenderest bonds and would remain so always, weighing and encouraging each other's prospects, every endeavour or resolution cemented by affection.

James had left the Army and, having been returned as Tory Member of Parliament for Fife, was mostly at Balcarres, while Anne in the south, acutely sensible of Coutts's 'infirmity of character', could still write of feeling inclined to make an idol of him. She was obliged to restrain her love for him with all her power; that he was too much her companion to be in awe of her, she was aware. Consequently when the child was sent off to school where he was no longer dominant, the triumphs of childhood years gave place to deficiencies of character, indolence and carelessness being the main misdemeanours.

The Reverend George Kyloch Rusden kept an establishment for boys at Leith Hill Place, Dorking. This was a large manor house structurally on the decline, but chosen for its having had their cousin, Lord Lindsay, as a pupil ten years previously. Mr Rusden was a conscientious man and at the end of the Michaelmas term acquainted James by letter of Coutts's progress in the early stages of Latin and copper-plate handwriting. This was endorsed by the recipient: 'Nothing particular. Regular tutor's eye.' Alas! by the summer of 1833 there was no hiding the fact that Coutts showed no habit of application, that his mind was upon a par with a child three years younger than himself, that he was lethargic, 'lolls and stares' over his sums, and of all things most reprehensible, he lacked 'manliness'. By July letters between the parents and Mr Rusden present the picture of a boy unused to applying himself to anything remotely difficult. As a child he had been read to before he could read words of one syllable; information had been conveyed to him in the most agreeable form without his having the trouble of working for it, whereas now Mr Rusden had to report that what he had learned and thoroughly understood one day he would not remember the next but would appear perfectly ignorant as if he had never heard or read one syllable on the subject. At times so great was his want of energy of thought that one would gather from his answers to questions on the very simplest subjects that he had never had anything explained or had the least instruction given him, 'and what is worse', continued Mr Rusden, 'he seems not to care whether he appears ignorant or not.' To a practising and strictly religious family it was at least of some comfort to learn that Coutts was attentive at his prayers and read the Bible in which he took pleasure.

In his holidays he continued to be a 'dear delightful plague' to his mother but again at school there was the necessity of rousing him to be 'more manly', though his lolling manner was not so troublesome and he was more 'gentleman like', ate better and yawned less at lessons. It seemed doubtful how far severity would be useful to so imaginative and volatile a mind and his father considered that he would require to be ridden with a light hand, sharp bit and spurs. It was particularly distressing to find his son unable to read fluently at the age of ten and his spelling to be a catastrophe on the grand scale. This was a circumstance that followed him throughout life. Among many strictures the Colonel singled out his habit of indolence '*of a most fearful nature*', following it up with a criticism of his eating 'very unneatly' and *stooping* as much as always although told of it ten times a day. Mr Rusden was still reporting utter carelessness and egregious blunders but Coutts seemed more contented if left to himself, sitting over the fire without doing or apparently thinking of anything, and evincing similar proofs of indolence and apathy.

However, the boy made a good impression on his godmother, Harriot Duchess of St Albans, and was the richer for it by one thousand pounds. Once an actress, the Duchess first married Thomas Coutts and inherited a vast fortune at his death. She had subsequently married the 9th Duke of St Albans but was to leave her first husband's wealth to his great-niece, Angela Burdett.[3] On this present occasion, while in Scotland at the end of 1835, she asked Anne to bring Coutts to see her and the generous present was effected. Dressed for her birthday dinner, resplendent in purple velvet, white feathers and diamonds, it appeared to Anne that unless she made a change in her mode of life she would not last long. Though unable to eat dinner, nevertheless at midnight she had an enormous supper of oysters, lobsters and whisky toddy, while during the day she seldom drank less than from two to three bottles of sherry as well as a quantity of wine and water. Indeed, her death was fairly imminent; she died eighteen months later.

3
Too Liberal a Dosage

School discipline in England had been ineffectual so a tutor for Coutts was engaged. On their leaving Scotland they were to spend a couple of days at Brondesbury on their way to Versailles where lodgings were to be found and the boy entered in a day school to acquire some French. Writing to Sir Coutts Trotter from Balcarres, James explained this new plan and begged him not to take an aversion to Mr Boyd, the tutor, for he had a thousand good qualities, though '*in point of manner* a vulgar man although not so mentally'. From Versailles in the summer of 1837 Coutts wrote to his parents in Scotland saying he would be sorry to be blind to the good qualities of the other schoolboys, but 'they are very irreligious and think nothing of doing things forbidden in the Commandments. The most common expression is "*O Dieu*" which I do not like to hear at all and that which I do not like to hear also is the manner they curse.' This must have caused consternation at Balcarres, not because they might have feared their son was in a fair way to turning into a prig, but because of their very deep and strongly held religious convictions, abjuring swearing or calls to the Almighty. They were unostentatious in the strictness of these beliefs and in their moral rectitude, but such was the governing expression of their lives. James was forever exhorting Coutts to pray and to thank God for mercies, and the whole family were of like mind.

This communication followed Anne to Brondesbury. She had been summoned south by the fatal illness of her father. The process of crushing a very large and very hard kidney stone had exhausted an already feeble frame, leaving him with no strength to combat his final illness. Brondesbury was to be given up, the London house, 11 Grosvenor Square, was to go to Anne; it remained the family town house until the end of the century.

Consequently it fell to the Colonel to travel hastily to Paris in January 1838 following a report from Mr Boyd regarding Coutts's health. Leaving Anne and the three younger children with her widowed mother he found his son and tutor installed at the Hotel Bristol, rue du Faubourg St Honoré, with Coutts suffering from a nervous malady with some resemblance to epilepsy though now almost impossible to define. It consisted of convulsions, fainting fits, attacks of such violence that it required his father's utmost physical powers to prevent his injuring others as well as himself – all this while sitting on the hotel room carpet together, sometimes for a half hour at a time. Other characteristics were snarling, twitching of the face, then suddenly gnashing, tearing or destroying everything within his reach, occasionally barking like a dog and kicking convulsively. These attacks would end by his becoming insensible, sometimes saliva coming from his mouth. He would recover suddenly and appear unconscious of what had passed, resuming conversation where he had left off. On one occasion, having kicked Mr Boyd, he was asked by his father whether he had been aware of having done so. Coutts threw his arms round his neck and kissed him and said he had been aware but had been unable to help it and had recognized in that instant all he had done.

The illness appears to have begun with a slight bowel complaint for which a homeopathic doctor in Paris, Dr Roch, prescribed *nux vomica*, containing strychnine, a perfectly normal medication for such a complaint. Either the dosage had been wrong or the chemist had made too strong a mixture, or else Mr Boyd may have administered too liberal a dose; any of these errors could have led to fits. The appearance of hydrophobia caused James to think

Coutts might have been bitten by a mad dog. By now, however, Dr Hahnemann, the celebrated homeopathic doctor, had been consulted, for Dr Roch, alarmed at the mischief he had done, would not go near the patient. The Lindsays were keen followers of homeopathic treatment and the Colonel was relieved to be told that Coutts was neither epileptic nor insane but that he carried the seeds of both diseases. This information, which seems to have been unfounded, would have horrified Anne but perhaps she took comfort in a little homily from her husband. 'Reflect for one instant', he wrote to her, 'that whatever affliction it pleases our beloved Father in Heaven to send us, it is our duty to bear it with calmness and resignation and to bless, as long as we can utter it, His Holy Name.'

A new medication, a 'smelling dose', was now administered which instantly brought on more violent fits but in the end seemed effective. Mr Boyd was kept hurrying back and forth to Dr Hahneman with reports, while Mrs Hahneman made the journey in reverse, bearing extortionate demands in the way of fees for her husband.

During this unhappy time for all three (Mr Boyd was devoted and helped in every way), whenever Coutts showed interest James would attempt different means of conveying knowledge. Apt with his pencil, Coutts would be encouraged to draw scenes for a little theatre he had made; geography was another possibility with the outlining of maps. It was hoped that passages from Wilberforce's *Practical Christianity* might make a thorough and lasting impression, although they watched carefully never to fatigue or give him more than *what he feels hungry for*. It was a matter for thankfulness that Coutts's mind was 'imbued with holy thoughts' and James prayed daily that he might be permitted to sow seeds of righteousness in the youthful mind, so that at some future day he would be fit for 'his removal from this life at that period which God thinks fit to call him'. (There were to be seventy-five years before the call came.) Meanwhile Coutts was allowed *Waverley* in the evenings.

This had necessarily been a lonely time for James, relieved only by letters to and from his wife. But as the boy slowly recovered plans were made for Anne and the children to come out and join him, though even now whenever he and Coutts went for walks a coach had always to follow them in case he had further fits.

By April the family was in Grosvenor Square, though not for long. A protracted stay in Italy was arranged. This would be a means for Coutts to recover his strength and, of some importance to the Lindsays, a form of economy. His father having died, Balcarres now belonged to James; repairs were necessary and a fair amount of building required to enlarge the house. Cheaper foreign living would solve the question of expense while at the same time it would open the children's eyes to other modes of life, to new attractions of architecture, art and landscape. To both parents with their keen artistic sense it would be a time of lively enjoyment.

4
Introduction to Italy

The Lindsays, with their equipage of tutor (Mr Boyd), Miss Jones (governess for the girls), Anne's maid and a courier, reached Rome at the end of the summer of 1838. George Richmond had been there a year already. His friendliness and vitality ensured him commissions and a ready place in society – unlike his lifelong friend, the artist Samuel Palmer, visionary and mystic. The Shoreham years behind him, Palmer and his bride had come abroad with the Richmonds. Despondent and of a highly nervous temperament, harassed by Linnell, his father-in-law in England, he found his poverty a bar to society and so to attracting employment. One wonders if the Lindsays ever caught a glimpse of this shabbily dressed genius, who suffered most dreadfully from the cold in winter and was frequently hungry, for his dislike of Italian cooking was severe. 'There is nothing portly in it,' he complained, 'nothing majestic or profound.'[4]

Lord Lindsay's arrival in Rome early in the following spring delighted his cousins. The children looked on him as one of their own family; he in turn reciprocated this devotion and it could be called the beginning of Coutts's introduction to what was to become the direction of his life: art and his own artistic capacity. Since a child he had used his pencil to communicate, however unskilfully, anything that captured his imagination. During his illness in Paris crayons and paper were a solace in the tedious hours spent indoors and his parents had encouraged his enthusiasm. There was to be no public school; his health precluded any formal education. He was destined for the Grenadier

Guards and meanwhile this loved and loving cousin provided a more gentle form of instruction.

Lord Lindsay at twenty-seven was still a bachelor, though within ten years he would marry Minnie, Coutts's eldest sister. Introspective, profoundly religious and retiring by nature, he lived – when not travelling abroad on some scholarly pursuit – with his parents at Haigh Hall near Wigan in Lancashire, where Lord Balcarres owned iron and coal property. His interests were many and varied: his understanding of art and aesthetics was only marginally subordinated to the vast knowledge and enthusiasm he brought to his lifelong collecting of books. This had begun at an early age and had continued with ever-increasing zest. His preoccupation was with the great Lindsay library, the celebrated *Bibliotheca Lindesiana* formed at Balcarres by his ancestor, David Lord Balcarres, and nurtured at Haigh till it reached its pre-eminence many years later. His influence on Coutts at this time was gradual but would be fully realized in two or three years. Now he showed his delight in joining his cousins by commissioning the Richmond portrait.

The likeness to the sitters was said by their mother to be very exact. Each figure carries its own individuality, while all were bound in a common affection. Coutts is totally absorbed in translating the scene before him onto paper. In the foreground, May, the prettier of the two sisters, kneels beside her brother leaning upon Richmond's mahlstick, and looks out at him as if for approval. Besides her love of music she too showed early skills in drawing and would have been sensitive to the artist's desire for a harmonious composition. With characteristic independence, the five-year-old Bob kneels slightly apart, his youthful face showing traits of the handsome man he will become. And in the centre of this portraiture – as in life – Minnie stands, tall for her age (all the family grew to be tall like their parents) but not yet 'out', indicating in her demeanour as she glances at her little brother, all the serenity and sympathy of an engaging and steadfast nature.

The sojourn in Italy, which included Paestum and Naples (for searching out books), helped to set up Coutts constitutionally; but when they moved to Ouchy, near Lausanne, for the summer Colonel James felt compelled to write a severe homily to his son, who though awake to the innumerable beauties of art and nature was only too indolent and indifferent on matters that failed to interest him – traits that had to be overcome. The fact that he was far backward in his education compared with his sister Minnie and others of his age was a handicap which only hard work would improve; so a tutor, Dr Ulrich, to succeed Mr Boyd, had been engaged. James told his son that he had taken such steps as were necessary to place him in due time in the Army, but until Coutts had acquired an education suitable to his rank and station and equal to any situation he might be called to fill, he would not allow his name to go forward. If by good behaviour he gained his father's confidence he would be treated according to his merits. His mother feared that when he came to manhood he would make very few friends and that knowing neither much of books nor much of mankind he would feel himself in an awkward position. Coutts must have put some energy into his conduct for when the family took a boat to Vevey and the Castle of Chillon he assumed the management of the party, 'made the bargains, paid the boat and did all very well'.

Another year was passed in Italy, chiefly in Tuscany, where they rented the Villa Torregiani in Florence, and it was not until the autumn of 1840 that Coutts returned to England with Lord Lindsay. They went immediately to Leamington, the one to take the water cure, the other, Coutts, to stay with his paternal aunt. There he found a strongly Evangelical household with his aunt interested in a number of religious institutions, particularly a local one for servants 'out of a place', according to Coutts, but more likely for a Home for Fallen Women. One evening a Baptist minister called and with a like-minded small company of friends spent the whole time in religious conversation, ending with extempore prayer and psalm-singing. The ridiculous language they conversed in, the nasal twang of the singing and the idol-worship paid to the minister quite sickened Coutts. 'In short,' Lindsay wrote out to Florence, 'if Coutts had not previously inbued those sound religious principles for which under God he has to thank James and yourself, that week at Leamington must have been hurtful to him.'

5
Encouragement and Stricture

While his family were in Italy Coutts made his home with
Lord and Lady Balcarres at Haigh and it was now that he
was much influenced by the admiration shown by Lindsay
for his successful, if youthful, attempt at figure composition. This admiration which would eventually lead him to
an artist's career, though excessive, was not altogether
misplaced, even if little help in disciplining his tendencies
towards idleness and indifference. To see Coutts with
Lindsay's eyes as he recorded to Anne a description of a
large cartoon Coutts had lately made, is to see him as a
near-genius. Its subject was an incident in *The Lay of
Hildebrand*, an eighth-century fragment of Old German
poetry, which captured the moment when father and son
paused in their fight by a battlemented castle in open
country with hills and trees in the distance and the army of
the Ostragoths and Huns winding through a mountainous
pass, horses caracoling. Even the expression of the two
warriors (the figures six feet high) was conveyed, as also the
family likeness in spite of their difference of age.

It is really quite in the spirit of the old Masters [Lindsay wrote],
and done in fresco would be beautiful. Here are we, striving to
revive the spirit of the past and restore the arts to their pristine
dignity and artists to a sense of their true vocation – but where (in
England) shall I find the man to follow up my views – who will be
my disciple? who will set the example? I want a man independent
in every sense of the term – why, *Coutts is the man*: give him only
fair opportunities – enable him to acquire mastery over the
mechanism of the art both in oils and pencil – store his mind well –
and with the knowledge of human nature he will acquire in active

life, and the inspiration of his own noble and Christianised heart within, – with his singular talent for observation, and his equanimity (so seldom united in genius) I see no earthly reason why he should not be a second Benozzo Gozzoli – aye, or rival to any one whose name we may rank still higher on the scale of excellence, and it would be a glorious vocation – how much good might thus be effected.

In Florence this letter was treated with reserve. Outwardly, Coutts was once more the golden boy of his earlier years: the looks, the bright hair, the boyish charm – soon to become something more devastating – the loving nature, the adored eldest son, sweet-tempered, well-mannered. But his parents were well aware of his extreme self-centredness.

That he had been spoilt as a boy there is no doubt, and having mixed with none but his family he had little or no understanding of human nature; his 'equanimity' was more a passive endurance, the result of a lack of interest. In future years Lindsay would realize and regret his extravagant appreciation of Coutts's merits but now he acted in what seemed the proper manner for gaining the boy's attention. Every day a portion of Gibbon was enjoyed; this was followed by an hour spent looking over some prints or books. Outlines of ancient geography, of Gothic and Hindoo mythology, were in prospect, Arabian history, architecture, literature, and also the history of the English language and studies of the modern discovery of the world. To these Coutts responded with enthusiasm. These subjects, though impressive in themselves, were scarcely an appropriate training-ground for a future in the Guards.

In appearance he was beyond his age. His health, though he denied it, was not yet stable. He disliked the prospect of being sent for a daily hour's ride, but when it came to it he quite enjoyed being on horseback. Lord Balcarres thought the blinding headaches from which he suffered, though of short duration, were occasioned by his stomach rebelling against his 'propensity to eat and drink too much and a

great love for a variety of trash (biscuits, fruit &c).' He
needed to study under a steady and able tutor to keep him
mechanically at work – a thing Coutts dreaded. 'I never saw
a more amiable, good-tempered young man - always ready
to do the wishes of those he looks up to, and tractable
though easily dashed and then rendered incapable of
action.' He thought Coutts was afraid of his father and
warned James that his own son, Lindsay, had also little
knowledge of men or intercourse with the human race and
Lindsay's partiality led him to cherish 'a feeling that Coutts'
mind will one day burst its cerements with a brilliancy little
expected by friends. You must not expect him to turn out a
brilliant man.' That his son should turn out a responsible
and God-fearing man was sufficient for James and as Coutts
struggled through adolescence he wrote him by way of
encouragement – and here there are familiar echoes of
Philip Gosse's strictures to his son Edmund[5] – 'The greatest
blessing which I now enjoy is the thought that you are a
child of God, that you really *adore* and *heartily* love Christ
who was crucified, who died to save you and that your mind
is imbued with faith, hope and charity. You feel you are a
sinner and seek His help.' At the same time he was writing to
Lord Balcarres to keep Coutts 'regular and *punctual*; on all
occasions the contrary habit is the bane of all the rising
generation – late in all things, irregular, cannot be depended
upon. It is a fault which renders negative all good intentions
and good qualities.' (A refrain echoed through time from
one generation to the next.)

6

Midwife to Coutts

Balcarres had been empty for close on three years so that building might progress while economies were made abroad to pay for the work of a greatly enlarged house. From Haigh Coutts journeyed north in early June shortly before the return of the family. It was a place he loved and even when forced to abandon it, largely because of the vicissitudes of his married life, it remained constantly in his thoughts and affection.

The property had been acquired in the late sixteenth century by a Lindsay who built the house of yellow sandstone on falling ground facing south, three miles from the Fife coast and commanding a spectacular view of nearly the whole stretch of the Firth of Forth and the Lothians beyond. Additions and variations in height detach it from the type of gaunt Scottish castle; twenty years later Coutts would again add to its size but at present James's ample enlargement with its small turrets echoing those of the early building and its gabled, crow-stepped extensions, a familiar domestic feature in Scotland, gave a balanced unity to the house which was now ready to receive the reunited family.

The gardens had not yet been laid out (this would be a later addition of his own), but as Coutts approached the house through the park he found the Persian lilac in full bloom, sheets of honeysuckle, and the rhododendrons at their best. Reporting to his father on the state of the house, he was full of enthusiasm. The new entrance and corridor surpassed anything he had visualized, being 'peculiar and most graceful' – in fact the spacious corridor was more like one in an Italian villa. His decorative tastes were developing and he begged his father not to put an inch of wallpaper on the walls as this would change its character immediately, as would carpet on what should be polished floor. The 'good old diningroom' looked venerable and the new library was handsome and cheerful. All in all, the building and improvements were a great success. With the family's return there was general rejoicing, particularly so over the pleasant effect Anne's fine old Italian furniture – newly bought – added to the embellishment of the rooms.

It was a delight to be home again but by the end of the year they were once more on the move. Minnie had been ill and her parents took her to Pau to regain health and strength; the two younger children went with them. Coutts meanwhile was to accompany Lindsay in a three-month stay in Italy and it was this unrivalled opportunity to study and learn under his cousin's guidance which defined his critical judgement and finally determined his future path.

Perhaps as he grew to manhood this is where his fascination lay. He made no progress into scholastic disciplines that did not interest him, but his sensibility towards history and literature and his understanding of art and facility in drawing were impressive. He could discourse with authority, adding a mixture of sophistication and youthful ardour which, allied to a charm of manner, was very attractive. When, later, he engaged upon what was considered a Bohemian attitude to life, he was no less captivating. Still, a streak of egotism and an inability to spell continued to exercise his parents.

The departure from England was chronicled by Lord Lindsay. A beefsteak at Rochester and the opportunity of visiting the Cathedral was a short stage on their way to Dover in the britska, the 'easiest goer' imaginable, with an additional projecting eave on the hood which completely excluded rain and rendered the windows unnecessary. These were removed, thus lowering the hood and enabling Coutts in the dickey to lean over and chat with Lindsay and his brother, Colin, the third passenger. During the day-time, which Lindsay spent in reading, he needed elbow room and Coutts was too 'portly' to sit inside, but after dusk, or if raining, he would join the other two and they could muddle all together most comfortably.

Soon after arriving in Rome Coutts learned with genuine delight that he had been commissioned to an ensigncy in the Grenadier Guards with two months' leave ahead of him, after which he would be doing duty at St James's. He was anxious to make the most of the time at his command and wishing to increase his knowledge of Italian, he read Tasso with an Italian master, an intelligent man, simple-mannered to a singular degree (according to Lindsay), with a strong religious feeling (according to Coutts). With his drawing master ('full of enthusiasm and pure feeling') he had worked assiduously every day and on dark winter afternoons copied statues in the French Academy from casts. It seemed to his cousin that Coutts's mind had all along gone in advance of matter and was expanding every day; his observations on all he saw were so just and true, his sentiments 'so broad and manly', that he proved an admirable companion. He propounded and absorbed new ideas, but – and once again the recurring phrase – his spelling was his great difficulty, of which Coutts was as aware as any.

A week in Naples (from where Colin, suffering from a 'nervous derangement', took a passage home) was spent searching out Neapolitan fresco painters contemporary with Cimabue; a day at Pompeii convinced Lindsay that 'three hours there are worth a week of ordinary study'. Returning to Rome Coutts told his father that he had bruised his toe, sprained his back and had suffered a series of headaches but his drawing had improved, the drudgery was over and that Lindsay had already bought one hun-dred volumes which were soon to be sent home, together with a cast of the 'beautiful Psyche' in Naples and of a 'sweet captive amazon on the lid of a sarchophagus in the Capitol'.

By the end of February 1842 it was time to move northwards. Coutts had now had some schooling in Roman antiquities; Greek sculpture aroused his special interest. Following the path of other travellers, Lindsay and Coutts set out on their month-long journey to Florence, staying on their way at Orvieto (for the Signorelli frescoes), at Spoleto, and at Montefalco (Benozzo Gozzoli). At Arezzo Coutts found a resemblance to the Elgin Marbles in the paintings of Piero della Francesca. By the time he had seen Assisi, Perugia and Siena, and had arrived at Florence with further treasures in store, his knowledge had been extended, his perceptions sharpened and in some branches his education intensified. A month later he sailed from Leghorn to England to take up his new duties. His cousin remained in Italy, missing his companion to whose mind, he conceded, he had acted as midwife.

7

The Guardsman

Soldiering was a life initially inimical to Coutts but by degrees he came to enjoy it, partly perhaps for its being the first time in eighteen years that he had escaped from the arms of his devoted family. He was to resign his commission in 1850 as his interests lay in other directions, but he nevertheless enthusiastically adopted military discipline – with himself in charge – at the time of the Crimean War. Still later, when married and with children, he twice took a small house at Aldershot to study new drill in operation in the Volunteer corps.

On this important milestone in his son's career, the colonel could indulge in some Helpful Hints. He was still at Bagnière de Bigorre, thirty-five miles south east of Pau, with the family. Known for its thermal establishment (founded originally it was said, by the Romans), the place was not without historical interest, having been once celebrated in the English wars of the fourteenth century and having connections with the exploits of the Black Prince.

Never short of affectionate, if rudimentary, advice, he had recommended Coutts to make the habit of rising early, to endeavour to abstain as far as possible from drinking wine ('heated blood makes a heated imagination'), to learn to say 'no' in a civil tone, to keep his letters safely locked up, for 'all servants read their master's letters', to make a large acquaintance with all the people in the circle in which he moved, for this was useful to a man and could later be of service to his fellow creatures. 'Do not shun society, but endeavour to discover the best.' If Coutts was wearied by these admonitions (few of which he observed) and he rarely showed signs of being so, he had the most fervent exhortation still to come. This was to read Blunt's *Pentateuch*[6] *before* he said his morning prayers as it would furnish him with numerous 'charming thoughts for prayer'. Finally there was the matter of his uniform and equipment and as Coutts was still growing it was inadvisable to get more than he absolutely required though what he purchased should be of the very best. Remembering that his regimental coat was to last him many years he was to have it made not according to fashion but according to correct regimental form.

Writing from Florence before his departure to England, Coutts had assured his father of two things, the one that he would never propose to a woman without first receiving his parents' permission, the other that, being aware that idleness was the highway to sin, he would not, 'with God's assistance', be found at the gambling table or 'other obscene or bad haunts'. And so, on 10 April 1842, well stoked with resolutions, Coutts joined the third battalion of the Grenadier Guards. Shortly after, he was introduced at the Guards Club by a young man, short and dumpy, his hair flowing in smooth ringlets and his fingers covered with jewels. Ten or fifteen young men stood by the window playing 'the Devil's tattoo' on the plate glass; others beating their boots with silver-headed canes, talking and laughing in a decent manner, except for one who had evidently passed through 'a course of swagger in a squadron of heavies'.

In early letters to his father – he had promised to write every fortnight – Coutts spoke of recurring headaches caused by taxing work which made him languid in the evening; the field days were fatiguing and it was so hot standing under arms in the broiling sun that it made his hand tremble while writing. However, he had passed the examination of different drills, he was managing his bearskin, he had mounted guard three times on the Tilt at Windsor and had been reviewed by Prince Albert and the

Duke of Wellington and when presented to the Queen 'of course I kissed her hand'.

But his letter-writing became more irregular and though he was known to have difficulty in writing, his mother wondered despairingly how it could be conquered 'if he does not meet it manfully'. Lord Lindsay was outspoken in condemnation. There had been complaints of one kind and another from his grandmother Lady Trotter, and from cousins and relations, gentle complaints, but without exception blaming Coutts for lack of consideration, in-attention in points of courtesy, selfishness and even un-kindnesses, faults which in a young man of eighteen years might still be lightly reprimanded or overlooked, but not in this highly moral family where the father's precept to his son had been 'I will not have you fall short of the highest chivalry in your conduct'. Nevertheless, these faults added up to a general principle of self-indulgence which 'judged by the law of charity must be branded with reprobation'. Owing to his Paris illness and his want of public school education his difficulties and hindrances were acknowl-edged, but *Resolution* was what was needed and with very many pious recommendations Lindsay urged him to struggle against the demon of Bad Spelling and to reform, for 'alas, what is love without esteem?'

Anne had other preoccupations which were centred on Coutts's health and his companions outside the army. His headaches and difficulties in concentration were a legacy of the 1838 malady and Anne had encouraged him to follow Dr Quin's treatment (another celebrated homeopathic doctor) to correct his delicacy of constitution which ex-posed him to the most disagreeable kind of suffering – that which affected 'the head and thinking powers', as she called it. Moreover, Coutts had taken up with Monsieur Antoine Roche, known for his publications of French prose and poetry, who had come to London as a young man and founded an educational institute where his courses on literature, history and astronomy were much 'suivie par la jeunesse aristocratique'. So far so good and Anne could recommend him as a language master, but as a friend he should be avoided – though tactfully – as being 'unsound'. The society of foreign actors and actresses in which he mixed was dangerous, not to say debasing, the flowering corruption that hid itself under the society of foreign artistes must be strictly evaded. Coutts, who had been inclined to exclude his relations and was now called to reject Monsieur Roche and his theatrical friends, found nothing congenial in his brother officers with whom he was most unhappy. By September he was stationed at Manchester and going through the ordeal of general bullying because the fashion of the battalion was to get drunk and this he refused to do. To his father he wrote – his good sense and affection having reestablished communications – that his brother officers, fat greasy voluptuaries, continued to drink and gorge themselves with their pleasures.

From Manchester Coutts was repeatedly at Haigh whenever he got leave, if only for a night, and he and his faults were the subject of many letters to Pau. Lord Balcarres too had seen officers of the regiment who had told him that Coutts, never having knocked about as was the case with most boys, had in consequence a much too high opinion of himself and that when he first joined he would not mix with others, making them feel they were not fit company for him. By no means unpopular, he had shown many good points of character but it was said that he was not clean in his person, did not wash properly, would appear in an unburnished coat and was generally slovenly.

A further appeal from Lord Lindsay followed. Did he realize, one wonders, that it was in great part his early praise that had added conceit to Coutts's other faults? Selfishness, spelling and inattention were still the main grounds for complaint but the tide appeared to be turning in his favour, though his colonel, Colonel Home, was still of the opinion that Coutts had had little opportunity of mixing with those of his own standing and that what he required was more knowledge of the world.

Worldly knowledge may not yet have been Coutts's strong suit but he was sufficiently enlightened to have managed to leave Manchester without settling his mess bill. From Winchester, where the battalion was then stationed, James was informed that a brother officer had paid the bill and that it had been repaid but only after having been repeatedly reminded, and that now having left Winchester, Coutts again owed his mess bill to the amount of three pounds, six shillings and tuppence as well as eleven shillings and sixpence to a stationer. Colonel Home had felt he was doing James a friendly act in reporting to him this particularly unwelcome piece of news.

8
Coutts as Author

After a leave of some weeks spent in Florence, Coutts, on his return in the summer of 1843, was quartered at the Tower where, as he told his parents, he was the 'signior' ensign.

He was beginning to enjoy his life, for London offered a vast assortment of amusements and social entertainments for a young Guards officer of conspicuous good looks, from a distinguished background and whose manners had at last acquired the necessary polish. His mother was still furnishing him with advice to the effect that friends made in youth were more valuable than any he could make afterwards and yet, as soon as he showed a degree of interest, however slight, in some young débutante of the season met at a tea-party, his father was immediately in a fuss – a handsome dowry being as important as a well-connected family.

With regard to the Highland beauties, the Miss Macleods, who are certainly extremely pretty [Coutts wrote to his father], do not fear that I am in danger though they are the most agreeable girls in London. I took tea with them yesterday and played at cards afterwards with them till twelve o'clock, and came away with a heart as sound as a bell. Truly and seriously you need not be afraid of my running my head into any foolishness with the Miss Macleods who I have not seen more than three or four times since you left.

This was a comfort to his father who feared he had done unwisely in leaving Coutts in town 'leading an *idle life*'.

His cousin, Lady Sarah Savile, got him many invitations; he was a guest at the Carnarvons, the Chichesters, at Lady [John] Shelley's breakfasts and at balls given by the Duchesses of Buccleuch and Bedford. With barely time to sleep he had never felt better. His father, back in London, took him to the Summer Exhibition at the Royal Academy. James thought it 'below par with quantities of portraits of the most vulgar people, and at least a regiment of soldiers, who having seen their best days (old twaddlers now) think to live in futurity – alas for second childhood'. Another visit was to Tittenhanger to his father's aunt, Lady Hardwicke, and his cousins the Charles Cannings and Louisa Waterford. Together they went to Miss Angela Burdett-Coutts who received them most kindly. Like much of the London world James looked askance at the marriage of her dear and constant companion, Hannah Meredith, who had been treated as an equal and had very recently married a Dr William Brown of humble origin. Mrs Brown's position was now an awkward one. James reported that

The Doctor and his *cara sposa* sat conscious of their dignity in her [Miss Burdett-Coutts's] apartment. I hear that on the marriage day she gave Miss M [eredith] a draft of £30,000. There were three or four mangey fellows in the room, not such as ought to be there. What a strange history hers is. I have not yet solved the riddle and perhaps no one will. She is not looking well, talks of going to Kissingen, I thought she had better try the benefit of the first syllable instead of the three and remain at home with a husband.

Moving on to Windsor in the winter, Coutts celebrated his majority in February, took tuition in fencing and when in London learned to 'scate' on the Serpentine. In the guardroom at Windsor he had decorated the wall with a large fresco landscape painting and when early in 1844 the regiment launched into private theatricals Coutts had been called upon to paint the scenery. He went down with measles and his mother, still abroad, persevered in naming the many precautions he should take, including having any worn garments *baked*. She had heard this to be most efficacious.

For some time he had been writing a play, *Alfred*, a 'poetic drama', partly mythological, partly historical, the plot of which, interwoven with a troop of fairies, was a tale of Saxons and Danes and the abduction of a girl by a fierce chief in the Danish camp. Lord Lindsay considered it the first genuine English play of real merit written since the death of Shakespeare and his contemporaries, for Puritanism had knocked *them* on the head and the Restoration had brought in the French and classic taste from which he considered they were only just recovering. Coutts had yet to master the mechanism of drama-writing and he still occasionally made sad work with rhymes and rhythm, though at times nothing could be more melodious.

When the work had been completed Coutts had read it to a family gathering at Haigh and Lindsay had written out to Anne about it at the utmost length. The reply showed little enthusiasm for its being published, though this is what Coutts hoped for and to this extent Lindsay sympathized with his wishes, although the danger lay for a young poet in being 'made the Demi-God of a Mayfair coterie, the Apollo of a young ladies' idolatry'. Of all things, Lindsay cautioned against its ever being acted which, though a seductive thought, would be ruinous to Coutts, for of all dangers to a dramatic poet, too great a familiarity with the stage was the most dangerous of all. With this Anne would have heartily concurred. Moreover, she feared that publicity might follow publication and Coutts's simplicity of character be lost in too much intercourse with the London world. 'A poet must certainly not be a frivolous and gay Lady Killer,' she wrote, 'or he will not long be a poet.' But this, she was satisfied, was not his way. He should treat his muse as a dear sister and never allow her to go into bad company where her taste or morals might receive an injury. The wrangle continued for months, Lindsay advocating publication and Coutts bringing out all the arguments he could assemble, among them that his brother officers, with whom he was now on a happier footing, were expecting publication, some to laugh, some perhaps to approve, and that he could not afford to delay. (Lord Lindsay who thought poets 'were such milksops nowadays' was delighted to perceive 'the shell hardening on the young crab'.)

By June 1845 the decision had been taken and on the eighth of the month Coutts sent *Alfred* to John Murray with an accompanying letter from Lindsay. The play was refused, seemingly unread, whereupon it was sent to Longmans and on 26 July the *Athenaeum* gave it three columns of critical assessment observing that 'There is a charm which brings it into comparison with some of Shakespeare's most delicate creations.' A testing comparison perhaps, but it was an achievement of no small order for the work to win the approval that it did. By then Coutts was in the toils of another historical-poetic drama, *Edward The Black Prince*, 'a magnificent Christian subject and God prosper me as I write to his glory and that of my country'.

Some little while previously he had approached the artist William Mulready, whom he knew to be an able teacher, with a view to some private instruction. Mulready gave him a lesson in comparative proportions of the human figure and 'noticed my falts and showd me my defects', and had in every way been extremely kind and helpful. 'I do not know how to recompence him,' wrote Coutts to his mother in France, 'could you not bring something useful for him from Paris on your return.' This would not have been the kind of initiative to impress Anne. The Lindsays were not immensely wealthy neither were they lavish with their money and she was still scolding Coutts for 'muddling away money'. Her reaction was to think it much too soon to talk about making Mulready a present. By and by, when Coutts had known him longer, he might send him game from Balcarres and if Coutts was diligent the artist would feel an interest in him and the lessons would be on a footing of 'one gentleman to another' and, supposedly therefore, no cause for remuneration. Mulready's account book shows no payment from Coutts; abundance of game was perhaps sufficient reward for a few lessons.

There was always this vexed question of money shadowing the pleasures of Coutts's life. From this irritant he would only be free twenty years later because of Blanche FitzRoy, born in London, in Berkeley Square, while Coutts was enjoying his 'idle life' in the Grenadier Guards and his mother was scolding him from St Germain-en-Laye for not making friends with those who would be useful and agreeable to him and his sisters.

9
The Rothschilds

Up to a point the FitzRoys lived a life apart, independent, self-sufficient. But when in 1859 Henry FitzRoy died leaving a widow, Hannah Mayer Rothschild, and Blanche, a daughter of fifteen, they were a desolate, anchorless couple. The spark of life that for Hannah was extinguished by loss and bad health had not yet quickened in Blanche.

Fortunately there was no cause to strive after a livelihood. Mrs FitzRoy had been born to wealth. Her father, Nathan Mayer Rothschild, like his four brothers, had left his home in the Jewish ghetto of Frankfurt-am-Main to establish the family's banking house abroad and in 1799 had settled in Manchester as a cotton broker – and a successful one. Six years later he came to London, was naturalized, and took up his quarters at New Court, St Swithin's Lane, where the offices are today. Seven children were born of which Hannah Mayer was the eldest of three daughters; she had four brothers besides.

A proliferation of closely-knit cousins and her own immediate family ensured an essentially happy youth. A Hebrew master taught her the language of her fathers and at five years, with a propensity for music encouraged by Mendelssohn and Rossini, who were friends of her family, she began to learn to play the harp. This felicity was furthered by the gift of a tiny gold harp given to her by her father.

In Paris at her first ball when staying with her uncle, Baron James de Rothschild, she presented a delicious picture dancing the gavotte, adding a double *entrechat* into the steps, her delicate features of purely Greek type

enhanced by a brilliant complexion and a waist so small
that a man could circle it with his two hands. This was
precisely what Prince Edmond de Clary, a young Austrian
of formidable lineage, proposed to do. He begged her father
for her hand in marriage. 'No daughter of mine shall marry
a Christian,' was the curt reply and Hannah to her grief was
hurriedly bundled home. The scales, therefore, were heavily
weighted when in 1838 she met the Hon. Henry FitzRoy,
Deputy Lieutenant for Northamptonshire, Member of
Parliament for Lewes, younger son of the 2nd Baron
Southampton, and fell in love with him. It was fortunate for
her that her father had died, for her stubbornness of purpose might never have triumphed over his formidable opposition. As it was, the course of love ran anything but
smoothly, both families objecting to the marriage: Hannah
Mayer's with anger, and the more vigorously, seeing in its
consummation two categories of betrayal. During his
lifetime Nathan Mayer Rothschild had given his daughters
large sums and by his will each had received £100,000.
Now this step would alienate money from the closely inter-
married Rothschild families; it would be also a treachery to
her faith.

Henry FitzRoy was born in 1807; his father had died
when he was a child, leaving him no patrimony. He grew up
a handsome man, with black hair and very bright blue eyes,
upright in character but serious and rather lonely, depend-
ing on his elder brother for augmentation to his own slender
resources. But with the certainty of so distasteful a marriage
this was peremptorily withdrawn and good relations were
never restored during Hannah's lifetime.

The wedding ceremony at St George's, Hanover Square
on 29 April 1839 was a sad occasion. All branches of
Hannah's wide and inter-related family and its affiliations
with Montefiores and Cohens were unforgivingly opposed
to the marriage but could not prevent it. Hannah was of age
and had her own considerable fortune. Her determined

intention, so unexpected in a young woman nurtured in an atmosphere of discipline and obedience, had strengthened her resolve to withstand all predictions and admonitions – as twenty-five years later her own daughter would do – and in consequence only one of her family, her brother Nathaniel, had been in church to support her. Her mother accompanied her in the four-wheeler to the door, neither speaking to the other, and had left her there in her plain morning gown and bonnet to be married in the rites of the new religion she had adopted, that of the Christian faith.

10

The FitzRoys

It was to this couple that the heroine of this story, Caroline Blanche Elizabeth, was born on 19 September 1844 at 43 Berkeley Square. The confinement was as short as it was severe. FitzRoy, now a Lord of the Admiralty as well as an MP, described the fledgling baby as resembling a young lobster. A boy, Arthur, had preceeded her two years earlier and with this young family the FitzRoys moved into Upper Grosvenor Street, No. 42, which was to remain home until Blanche's marriage, followed within months by Hannah's death. Adoring her husband, whose jealousy when out walking extended to her having to keep her veil down to avoid admiring eyes, Hannah nevertheless felt the loss of her large Jewish family. Having made no friends of her own outside that all-embracing circle, she was lonely. In contrast to the strength of will that had supported her through her marriage crisis, she was now in almost constant 'delicate health'.

Blanche's first recollection at the age of three was in a rented cottage in Norfolk (with good shooting nearby), where lavender grew profusely in the garden and where the children's nanny always made them leave something on their plate: 'Always leave something for manners,' Blanche remembered. She was a red-cheeked, good-humoured child and when later, and by degrees, the FitzRoys began to be accepted by some of the Rothschilds she would remember with fury how her French uncles would pinch her cheeks, exclaiming: 'What rosy cheeks' – and she who had so wished to be pale and romantic! Worse still when they followed this up with

'Blanchy Blue
How are you?'
She hated her hard little plaited pigtails tied with brown ribbons, the doses of rhubarb and magnesia, the grey powders.

Autumn and winter were spent at Pau, the children and servants riding there in a cumbersome stage coach and the parents occupying the coupé in front. Blanche chiefly remembered it because of her terrible travelling costume, her close 'cottage' straw bonnet enveloped in a gauze veil, and her ugly cloth gloves.

There were visits to Brighton for the regular change of air, where the street cry of the muffin man was long remembered, the umbrella and chair menders, the Dutch girls who sold white brooms, the small shops on the Chain pier dealing in tiny red shells – all things to claim a child's attention – and the man who strode the streets singing while selling brandy-balls.

In London her father would take her for long drives in a hooded cabriolet to Hampstead and as a companion on the round of fashionable Sunday visiting, where the fascinating hostess Lady Waldegrave, in her large house, 5 Carlton House Terrace, would remain a memory to the child, of brilliance, culture and opulence. Lady Molesworth was another such. Born Andalusia Carstairs to a writing-master, she had been educated for the stage but having married the wealthy politician Sir William Molesworth, Bt, she had translated her skills and all her eccentricities into a life of relentless social advantage.[7] Her green parrot was probably, in effect, the precursor of Blanche's own dream – later achieved – of possessing one of this brilliant species.

At eight years Blanchy's many engaging childhood habits unfortunately coincided with youthful precociousness, as when her mother was obliged to tell her she was getting too old for kissing her hand to the butler as they drove off from the door. She had started to study Greek now and drawing, and had developed a passion for writing poetry; she pricked out the verses on a large sheet of drawer paper, having had her pencil and nightlight removed when she attempted to write her rhymes at night. When she attended a Court ball for children with her parents she had been driven to Buckingham Palace in a yellow chariot, the coachman in his wig on the box and two footmen up behind while she stood between her parents so as not to crumple her little white tulle dress. Her straight black hair had been loosened from its imprisoning pigtails and was crowned with a jasmine wreath.

Her father's appointment as Under Secretary for the Home Office in 1852 would have been a gratification had it not been for the tragedy that shadowed all their lives for the next six years. Arthur, the cherished only son, had suffered a riding accident when crossing Park Street from Upper Grosvenor Street. His pony had shied and had thrown the boy onto a heap of flint left there for the repairing of the road. His spine had been irreparably damaged, his suffering intense, and he was an invalid until his death in 1858 at the age of sixteen. Hannah Mayer found it difficult to face up to this life-in-death situation and the family became more and more inward-looking and self-absorbed and Blanche's life in consequence more restricted. Hopes centred on cures for Arthur. Dieppe, with gentle sea-bathing, was advised in 1855 but what Blanchy most remembered was her blue and red bathing-suit and the shame of her hideous oilskin cap. She was told of the fall of Sebastopol when standing outside a pastry-cook shop and the two were forever after inexorably linked in her mind. At Tours, to which they moved for Arthur's health, she had French lessons (in which language she remained fluent all her life) and though she did not much care for it her father taught her to ride while declaring that she looked like a sack of potatoes on horseback.

Dedication to Art

Following the potato famine in Ireland, Sir Robert Peel introduced his bill into the House of Commons in early 1846, proposing the repeal of the Corn Laws. London was in a ferment, 'even the Life Guards are not at a loss for a subject to speak on,' Coutts told his mother at the beginning of February, 'actually only one of them fell asleep after the cloth was drawn last night – this a great sign of stirring times.'

Still at Windsor, he discharged his regimental duties with enthusiasm and had been promoted captain. He hunted in Northamptonshire, had Italian lessons in which he was becoming proficient, and listed, for his father's benefit, the authors he was studying. As a would-be playwright, Massinger, Wycherly, and Hazlitt for his dramatic criticisms, were uppermost. But whether in France, in Italy, or at Balcarres, the Lindsays were watchful of their eldest son's conduct in society. There was no satisfaction whatsoever in learning of his 'great acquaintance with Mr Mackenzie, an editor of the *Times* newspaper'.[8] He was urged to select his friends from amongst the 'real old aristocracy': 'choose your friends rather to raise you than to sink you.' Of lesser interest, as they saw it as an encroachment on what they hoped might be a life of duty and service, were Coutts's determined efforts to succeed in play-writing and painting. To his mother he seemed to live a life without order in which it was not in his nature to carry through an undertaking to the end, a judgement reinforced with the years. A new thing would strike him and off he would go, abandoning the old. However, his historical drama *The Black Prince* was published by Longmans in the late spring and was much advertised. Lindsay had no doubt of 'Coutts's ultimate recognition as the poet of the age'. This was his last poetic drama publication. Those high ideals of youth were giving way to a slightly more disingenuous approach to life, unintentionally fostered by the strictures of his father and mother. He had never overtly showed impatience at these, but the allurements of manhood supervened. There had been the incident in which Coutts had admitted, not without a feeling of shame, in which he had lost thirty pounds in one night by gambling. The temptation had always seemed so distant that he had been almost unaware of what he was doing until, frightened by what he had lost, he had then continued playing, in an attempt to keep his secret.

Gambling, however, was not the only temptation to which he had fallen. A *folie de jeunesse* was no unlikely occurrence. There can have been few young and handsome Guards officers who had no pretty, youthful and willing damsel on the side, though perhaps not all found themselves launched into paternity as did Coutts. Lizzie Chambers, whose background is not known, had proved herself accommodating. The first child, George Chambers, was sent for education to the Classical and Commercial Academy, Vale of Heath, Hampstead in 1854, run by a Mr Lightbody. Mr Boyd, the tutor of earlier days, was instructed by Coutts to keep an eye on the child, while Lizzie Chambers, pretty and alluring, pops in and out of the story for a few years, clinging to the hope of marriage with her lover.

A marriage in the summer of 1846, not of Coutts but of Minnie, the loved eldest daughter and sister, was the immediate excitement and gratification. The family had returned to Grosvenor Square from France in May to launch her into society. In July she was married to Lord Lindsay at St George's, Hanover Square. He had loved her for many years and here was the perfect uniting of cousinship. After the wedding James, Anne, May and Coutts had gone to Kensington Gardens and sat on a haystack till nearly seven o'clock in the long summer afternoon. Then they went home and had tea in the old schoolroom.

By 1847, with Coutts once again quartered in the Tower, letters from Fontainebleau, where the Lindsays were staying, were full of sage advice and not without some curiosity. The hope of a marriage to bring him happiness compounded with material blessings was frequently in their minds. 'Coutts attends about seven balls a week. I trust, poor boy, he will one day find a happier and blissful employment for these hours with some companion worthy of his love.' Coutts was skilful in extricating himself from such questions as, from James, 'Tell me what young ladies you are flirting with at the west end of the Tower, whether because you are drawn into their train or because you cannot say no, or whether *con amore*.' Nor did the questions diminish his affection for his parents. His mother would always remain a close and beloved figure, later one of the serious stumbling rocks in his marriage. But much as James grumbled about his son, even to complaining that Coutts had intended joining a 'Balloon party'⁹, and was indeed the instigator of the plan ('What lunatics they are to run the risk of being made cripple for life to say "I have been up in a balloon"'), he still thought him a 'fine and manly fellow', as did those with whom he consorted. Gone now the faulty manners, the effects of bad health, the carelessness of behaviour. His attractions were many, not least the original mind which flourished in congenial company. His was a distinctly artistic personality, ardent in one so relatively young (he was twenty-four) and, for his time, singular that so professional an approach to painting was to be found in one whose future would have seemed to be committed to the managing of a Scottish estate and following in the paths of his forebears. His appearance was attractive, and the indefinable charm of which he was still unconscious exerted a fascination that remained to the end of a very long life. But by then there were diverging characteristics. As his mother had represented in earlier years, the 'lack of patience and steadfastness which marked his career throughout' had extinguished the bright promise of his youth. His labours were never to be crowned with a lasting success.

This all-absorbing devotion to a life of painting brought his decision to a head in February 1850; on his twenty-sixth birthday, he resigned his commission in the Guards. He had reached this conclusion after some deliberation, aware that it might grieve his father. His young brother Bob, however, would get a commission with the Scots Fusilier Guards later that same year and this would lessen any opposition to his scheme. For his scheme was this: his life was his art, Italy his inspiration. The one would be auxiliary to the other. Since youth he had been influenced by his cousin, now his brother-in-law, who had recently published his distinguished work on *The History of Christian Art*, placing him immediately in the forefront as an interpreter of Christian philosophy and, as would be called today, an art historian. Ruskin, at the age of twenty-eight, gave the work a long and analytical report in the *Quarterly Review*. Lindsay's estimates of the various schools and masters were the views of a scholar and a man widely travelled. Coutts had given careful attention to these volumes, which were integral to his desire of dedicating himself to the study of art.

Still closely united in affection, the family was now scattering. Bob was doing his training in the Army; Minnie, living at Haigh and raising her children, still found time to help her husband in his unremitting pursuit of further rare publications for the expansion and enhancement of his library. In 1849 May was edging towards matrimony. A fervent suitor was Lord John Manners, second son of the

5th Duke of Rutland. There seemed to be everything in his favour ('a religious man') except that being only a second son, though heir presumptive, the suggested financial provision for a wife and possible children – the pivot on which the alliance hung – was thought to be inadequate by May's parents. Coutts's opinion was sought before the subject had been broached to May, though she can scarcely have been totally ignorant of what was then afoot. Coutts, at Windsor, impartial though he tried to be in a long and solicitous letter with occasional misspellings, came to the conclusion that 'if £1600 a year be secured for them and their children at his marriage and that sum be settled on May in case of his death, for her life', then he was in favour. 'If Lord John were allowed to try his chance, that means "Yes", for the moment he crosses Balcarres door the thing is settled.'

The chance was not given him. There were insufficient means to settle on any children in the case of the loss of both parents and it fell to James to impart this unfavourable conclusion. Lord John behaved in exemplary manner, praying that 'every blessing may light on the head of her who is denied me, is and shall be the prayer of him who is Yours very truly . . . ' The proposal was repeated in the summer of 1850 and Minnie wrote distractedly to her parents begging them to 'decide against it a second time', on the grounds that the more she saw of her sister the more sure she felt that she would not be happy with a poor man. Begging her mother instantly to nip all hope in the bud, she felt it cruel to give the wooer false hope and for May 'the pain of refusal against her own wishes'. This is the only indication of May's feelings, elaborated by Walburga Lady Paget's pen in 1928 when, in referring to Anne ('a real old campaigner') as having insisted on her daughters marrying rich men, she hazarded the information that May in her youth had passionately loved Lord John Manners but that some estrangement had arisen; that years later in sorting through family letters she had come upon his to her father asking for her hand and this letter had been suppressed.[10] Lord John (who subsequently became 7th Duke of Rutland) married soon after and within a few years May's marriage to one of the wealthiest commoners in England delighted her family.

Shortly before this domestic drama had unfolded, the sisters and brothers had spent a fortnight together in early August at Dunecht, in Aberdeenshire, a property recently bought by Lord Balcarres as an investment and handed over to his son. Coutts had arrived with a friend, Francis Cust, and the two had reappeared in correct Highland attire, Coutts looking very handsome in his kilt, but May, writing to her mother at Vichy, thought Mr Cust's legs did not bear inspection. The two friends had started off for Loch Skene, returning with snipe and an Aberdeen duck – 'alias, a partridge' – at which the keeper had turned up his eyes (this was 1st August) and looked the other way. They had met a couple of old women who had hid themselves on glimpsing these two outlandish figures, not seen thereabouts since the days of the Picts, and a little girl had stood trembling by the roadside at the sight of them.

It had been an interlude of happiness often referred to by the brothers and sisters for it would be some time before they were all gathered together again.

12

Abroad and at Home

The 1850s were years of the most pleasurable enjoyment. After six years in the Army Coutts had now the freedom of choice in his mode of living. He chose that of the dilettante in which painting and an intuitive knowledge of art would take priority. In consequence of having had no conventional training of the mind which a disciplined education would have brought him, his powers of concentration were limited and his family had resigned themselves to his mercurial habits, for with no settled occupation, no responsibilities and no necessity to form any anchorage other than to suit his own pursuits, he seemed, as Minnie confided to her sister:

Like some beautiful many-branching flower which struggles all over the bed . . . and a good gardener would tie these branches to a stake and so form a beautiful mass of colour and stand firm and united. What Coutts wants is that stake.

But destiny, all unknown, was supplying his need (though it would take him twenty years to find it) in the form of a baby girl, Harriet Kate, born to William Burfield, servant, and his wife, at Brighton in April 1850. For the present she was as distant from Coutts's imagination as was Blanche FitzRoy, the child being schooled in all the virtues, niceties, and accomplishments comprehended in the anticipation of a brilliant match. But it would be Kate, now an infant, who would capture and retain his lasting devotion, first as model and mistress, then as mother of his son and, after prolonged waiting, eventually as his wife.

For Coutts, the initial consequence of his resignation

from the Army was a journey to Italy, staying for a while in Paris in order to study in Ary Scheffer's studio and under his direction. The artist was an old and dear friend of his own and of his parents and had made portraits of his father and his maternal grandmother. In his day Scheffer's reputation was greater than that of Ingres and to Coutts he seemed an artist of European fame and influence. He set him so high in his estimation that even Giotto, Fra Angelico, and Raphael were, in comparison, limited in their range of variety of expression.[11]

From Civita Vecchia before embarking for Naples he wrote to his father of a ride through the ilex avenue at Castel Gondolfo in moonlight while 'the blush of sunset' was hanging over the *campagna* and peasants were returning from a *fiesta* at Albano, singing and laughing 'as they strooled by'.

At home his unmarried sister May was enjoying her 'season'; her quick eye for comedy described a concert at the home of Angela Burdett-Coutts where the hostess looked overpowered by the enormous wreath of white flowers on her head and five rows of large diamonds around her poor little thin neck; and the magnificent Duchess of Sutherland, Mistress of the Robes to Queen Victoria, was a sight to be seen and to be wondered at, 'smiling so very graciously and looking so charming and condescending as she sailed past through the admiring crowds' crowned with a wreath of immense lilies and a very small daughter towed in her wake.[12]

In the spring of the next year, 1851, Coutts was again in Italy, at Genoa, Leghorn, and finally in Rome where he found himself quite embarked in the Roman society of the Dorias, Borgheses, Rospigliosis; Rome was also full of English, Lady Pakenham and son and daughter and others. His lodgings, to which he moved at Easter, were at 40 Via Gregoriana, twenty-five scudi a week, and he felt he could not have chosen better. His mother, once again in London for May's interest and to visit the Great Exhibition, wrote nostalgically to Coutts of the cork woods and the wild paths at Castel Fusano. 'I can shut my eyes and hear the branches of the woods waving and see the wild flowers and the arbutus', and on opening them again all she could discern was the yellow London fog.

However, it was not long before the Lindsays were themselves in Rome and it was there, at the end of the year, that James heard he had been promoted to general. Earlier they had tried to induce Coutts to join them for the winter, recounting the delights of the countryside and pleasantness of the society in which they found themselves. But he was not to be tempted from Scotland. That summer he had found Balcarres 'like a woman in full beauty where womanhood takes the place of youth', and the garden was blushing with roses and the trees superb in their emerald foliage. He had with him his brother whom he found indolent, with no habit of exertion – much as he himself had been at an earlier age. Bob was as silent as if his tongue were chained but this did not make his heart the less warm. From Scotland Coutts planned to spend the winter in London, have Bob with him, and to study without distractions. This was wholly alien to his mother's wishes. There would be no servants in Grosvenor Square and the brothers would be living alone 'in a slip shod manner' without an establishment, and Bob would never have so good an opportunity again of going to Rome, which in itself was part of education. They could have their own lodgings and be uninterrupted, going only to the family for dinner; if Coutts did not learn to work when there were some impediments in the way, his work would never be very useful.

Coutts overrode all these arguments and with Bob as a 'compagnon' took a lodging at Hampstead standing almost at the top of the hill, free from all smoke, looking to Highgate on one side, Willesden on the other. Out at seven o'clock they would take a walk before breakfast when

Coutts would find his surroundings half-veiled with light mists and sparkling in dew; he had no idea so much growth still existed in the close vicinity of London. 'Far prettier than Kew,' he thought. He had done well in his lodgings; Bob had praised everything and they were happy and content in every way. These months had been a kind of tutelage for Bob. Neither Eton nor the Army had done anything to break down his reserve and Coutts had hoped that by his influence and readiness to impart his views and offer information on a variety of subjects, he might, as he told Lord Lindsay, 'do for Bob as you once did for me', since he owed every good habit and all knowledge he possessed to his brother-in-law. But he was convinced that with his unreliable self-control and lack of application, Bob would have been unfitted to take advantage of a visit to Italy.

For the next year or two, except for an occasional trip to Paris (the fare standing at £1.4s first class return), Coutts was in England staying at St George's Drive, Pimlico, with a new friend, James Swinton, who was making his name as a fashionable artist in oils and crayon portraits of some of the great families; even now he had several commissions of which two whole-lengths had set him up in spirits and in purse. His portrait of James was considered a good likeness.

At the Travellers' Club Coutts was excellently posted to watch the procession of the Duke of Wellington's funeral wend its ponderous way to St Paul's Cathedral. As a mere sight it could not compare with many he had witnessed in Italy, but here 'everything was so well in keeping with the character of England and earnestness and truth, which was very fine', that he doubted whether any splendour could have increased the effect. By the end of the year he was at Wilton Street, Grosvenor Place, with Lord Gifford. Writing from Italy, his mother had mentioned with some reserve the sisters Lady Dufferin and Caroline Norton, whom she had encountered at Naples. Lady Dufferin had been widowed in 1841 and was now contemplating marriage with the young

Lord Gifford, son and heir of the Marquess of Tweeddale, an invalid and seventeen years her junior. Her son was showing marked attention to May. The sisters were the daughters of Thomas Sheridan, and the third sister, the Duchess of Somerset, had been Queen of Beauty at the famous Eglinton Tournament of 1839. Together they formed a remarkable trio but it was Mrs Norton who now attracted the most attention, not only by her looks (Anne could write with enthusiasm of her 'wonderful beauty') but also by her notorious recklessness. There had been the unsavoury law case in the 1830s when her husband had instituted proceedings against Lord Melbourne, the Prime Minister, as co-respondent for adultery with his wife. Lord Melbourne had been immediately acquitted but Caroline's reputation had never entirely recovered. She lived apart from her husband, was cut off from her children, had little money, wrote novels and verse and threw herself impulsively, and usually vociferously, into any issue in which she could argue her views. There is a suspicion that Anne was apprehensive lest Coutts be trapped by this unconventional and witty woman, who with her 'deep, rich, soft voice' and 'still gloriously beautiful face' might exert a formidable influence. But there were greater charms at work and these nearer home, for Coutts was to become acquainted with Virginia Somers, his cousin's wife.

13
Lady Somers

In 1850 this cousin, Lord Eastnor, heir to his father the 2nd Earl Somers, and to the London estates of St Pancras and Somers Town, had made a surprising marriage, not favourably viewed by his family or relations. His mother, Lady Caroline Yorke before her marriage, was one of three sisters, the Countess of Mexborough and Lady Stuart de Rothesay making up the trio. They in turn were daughters of the 3rd Earl of Hardwicke and his wife, daughter of the 3rd Earl of Balcarres. At the age of twenty-one Eastnor had been thrown from his horse opposite Apsley House when riding in the Row and had sustained some damage. This accident had affected a character already marked by extreme modesty which, combined with a natural laziness, provoked an indifference to public life or worldly success (though he was for six years Member of Parliament for Reigate where he owned property), and this despite a well-informed mind and gifted personality. A good draughtsman and painter in watercolours, he had known and remained friends with Ruskin since Oxford 1838 and through his influence had learned to appreciate Turner. He had wished to adopt painting as a profession but this his mother would not countenance.

In early autumn 1843 Eastnor had accompanied Layard, already a recognized explorer and soon to be known for his excavations, in his travels to the islands in the Aegean and to Mount Athos. Scholarly, well-read, of a genial disposition, Eastnor had fulfilled the part of the perfect travelling companion. Equally, he had journeyed with Robert Curzon, another well-known traveller in Turkey, this time to Greece, making sketches for Curzon's book, *The Monasteries of the Levant* (1849). His appearance, however, was against him. Born in 1819 and now in his early thirties, he was a man of low stature and to George Du Maurier's mind 'a jolly sort of little fellow' with a squeaky voice, and to his cousin Charlotte Canning's way of thinking he looked – not to mince words – 'too frightful', certainly in contrast to the beautiful girl he had married.

This was Virginia Pattle, the sixth of seven daughters of an Anglo-Indian family. The story of their father's undignified end as a corpse in a barrel of rum which burst in the ship's hold on its homeward-bound journey for burial from India to England, with the widowed Mrs Pattle and the two youngest daughters on board, has been too often told to need repeating. Virginia had been brought up in India and was said to talk in Hindustani with her sisters who numbered Sara Prinsep among them, the lion-huntress of Little Holland House, and Julia Cameron the celebrated photographer.

Violet Hunt, whose imagination and pen were as fanciful and irrepressible as her tongue, noted in her diary that the sisters' hair and complexion were 'nigger', as was also their lazy tolerance, and that in their dress the lack of shape and general tendency to sloppiness was inherent in all women with 'a touch of the tar brush'.

Known as Beauty, Dash, and Talent respectively (or Pattledom as a body), the two elder sisters were not good-looking women while Virginia, according to a great-niece, had the face of a madonna. Radiating goodness and with immense charm to complement her looks, she yet seemed unaware that passing this tall figure in the street draped in a long cloak, people would turn to stare. Her oval face was delicately poised on a slender neck, her black hair swept into a net, while heavy lids partly veiling her dark eyes endowed them with a mysterious hint of romance. The 'caressing kindness' of which the same great-niece spoke, and the insinuating manner, belied an irrepressibly impulsive character, tempered by a surprising shrewdness and an almost irrational determination which, when forcefully effected in opposition to her husband, could be rashly intransigent. Coming upon a whole-length portrait of her by G. F. Watts, her most devoted admirer, Eastnor fell in love with the sitter, managed an introduction, declared his love, while the consternation in his family did nothing to stem his ardour.

Charlotte Canning hoped her beauty and perfect manners would compensate for lack of fortune or a '*beau nom*', but her Christian name seemed by its impropriety an almost insurmountable obstacle in Victorian society. 'Oh, that she had another name,' exclaimed Charlotte. The marriage was finally settled and the wedding held at St George's, Hanover Square in October 1850.

For the first years Coutts saw little of them; their honeymoon journey took them to Portugal, complete with a quantity of sketch books and other drawing material. The first child, Isabella, was born in 1851 and before the birth of the second, Adeline, in the following year, husband and wife had been camping among Bedouin Arabs. Virginia, the child to die early, was born in 1855. Anne Lindsay considered the Somerses[13] to be people of most cultivated tastes, but writing to his mother that year (1853) Coutts remarked upon Lord Brooke's marriage to Lady Anne Charteris: 'I think her perfectly lovely', and commented upon her 'high-born' look in signal contrast to Somers's wife, 'not at all like a Pattle'. But this impression was not to last. Meeting frequently in the artistic world and claiming kinship, the two men had forged a link: Somers's appreciation and knowledge of painting drew him close to Coutts, while by Virginia Coutts had been instantly captivated. At the time of her marriage there had been some scepticism voiced by ill-natured tongues regarding her position in the social world in which her husband took his natural place. 'It

The Lindsay Children, Rome, 1839

Balcarres

Colonel James Lindsay, 1852

Robert Lindsay, 1854

Coutts Lindsay with Robert
Adamson, head gardener at
Balcarres, 1850s

May Holford, c. 1856

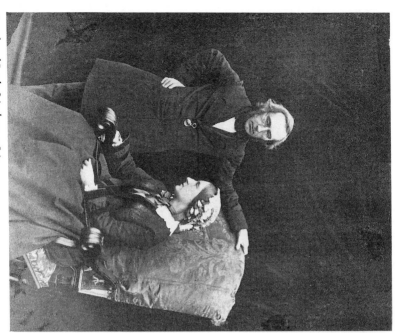

Lord and Lady Lindsay, 1860s

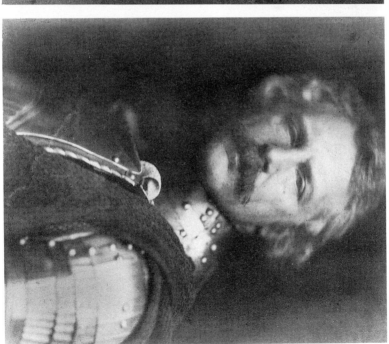

Coutts Lindsay in armour

Countess Somers, 1860s

Coutts and Blanche Lindsay, Balcarres, 1864

Blanche Lindsay, 1860s

Coutts Lindsay, c. 1865

Blanche Lindsay, 1874

will be curious to watch her rise, as I believe she is *not* yet in good society.' Any disadvantage she may have had to encounter soon vanished; at Carlton House Terrace and in Herefordshire at Eastnor Castle, the massive early Gothic revival baronial castle with turrets, bastions and battlements completed in 1820 by Robert Smirke, Virginia triumphed. For the next twenty years her influence on Coutts was predominant, even to choosing him a wife – which gossip said was to hide their own intimacy. But whatever their relations, and this is never clear, nor is Somers's perhaps ambiguous devotion to Coutts, the Somerses filled a considerable portion of Coutts's life, and so, equally, did he become a necessary factor in both of theirs.

Coutts was in London for the winter of 1853 taking lessons in oils once or twice a week with Charles Sibley; also studying with the painter William Leitch as his master, sometimes at the sumptuous newly-built, though as yet unfinished, Dorchester House in Park Lane, belonging to the wealthy collector Robert Holford. He was drawing several hours a day, principally from the Elgin Marbles and making outlines of anatomy; often Leitch ('a most charming compagnon and a pattern of energy') would join him in the evenings and they would draw from models. Anne, in Balcarres with Bob, who had suffered some damage to his back and was now convalescing, looked unfavourably on Coutts drawing from life in the evenings, conjecturing that if he drew 'those vile coarse models he would destroy his taste since he would be unable to idealize them'. Further, she suggested he should ask to see Virginia Somers's drawings, 'they are not pretty but very fine, bold and graphic like a man.'

Anne wished Coutts would join the family party at Balcarres consisting of James, Minnie and her husband, May, and of course Bob, to entertain whom she had devised the scheme of pasting small drawings on to a seven-foot-high, five-fold screen, a border of red cut velvet running the length of the base. By the time it was completed in 1859 there were over three hundred watercolour drawings, with Coutts supplying some fifty-five and his mother and sister May hot competitors. The family had been urged to contribute. Once the screen was started, others applied to assist, for numerous additions were needed to cover one panel. Entreaties for contributions continued for several years. Fortunately the gifted Louisa Waterford who proudly offered a drawing was never to know that Coutts did not admire it. As the screen stands today (owned by a member of the family) it represents a delightful and artistic enterprise.

While urging Scotland, Anne begged a little budget of news for her husband. Coutts preferred London and its attractions (of which Lizzie was still one) but sent a description of a dinner at Swinton's, whose sister proved taciturn and Lady Eastlake, the only other guest, had provided most of the conversation. As the wife of the President of the Royal Academy Coutts found her company congenial, in spite of the air – 'imperial in manner, language, and dress' which tended to lower her to 'just short of one of the most agreeable women' he had ever met. He voted her 'altogether a very grand creature' who moved her head '*a guisa di leone*' and spoke like the queen of beasts. Meanwhile, still at Balcarres, at the start of the new year, 1854, Anne was engaged in reading Benjamin Haydon's *Life** and was deeply affected by his sad struggles for celebrity though gauging that his pictures must have been vastly inferior to his own estimation of them; never had she read a more melancholy book. The pleasant interlude at home was shattered when news came that Bob was ordered with his regiment to the Crimea. The family gathered in London and Coutts's first step was to make over to him the saddle and bridle he had had made for an intended

*The Autobiography and Memoirs of Benjamin Robert Haydon, ed. Tom Taylor, 1853.

expedition to Spain but which were built for the type of horse also used in Turkey. His second action was to make a portrait of Bob for their mother, but with only two short sittings he was unable to draw more than a slight chalk sketch. With this, however, he established the truth of Anne's praise of a few months earlier regarding Bob's superb good looks, which when set upon a tall and well-proportioned figure likened him to a Donatello or a model of a warrior saint.

14
The Pleasures of Rome

Bob sailed with his battalion in the middle of February, taking with him the hopes, fears and love of all the family, but fortunately for those remaining there was a romance in the making to occupy much of their thoughts. May, who had never lacked for suitors and could number Sir Thomas Erskine, Lord John Manners and Lord Dufferin among them, had fixed her heart upon Robert Holford, a man more than twenty years her senior, a connoisseur of art, a multimillionaire since the age of thirty, and the happy possessor of an income of £35,000, and of Westonbirt, a property in Gloucestershire. Here was a man who 'in his ordinarily entirely comfortable completeness' Anne found very good-tempered and pleased with everybody and everything about him.

Having the means to form an impressive library and a magnificent collection of pictures, he had acquired paintings by, among others, Titian, Veronese, Tintoretto, Rembrandt, Vandyck, and sketches by Rubens. To hang these canvases in a noble setting he had engaged Lewis Vulliamy in 1848 to make designs for a new house in Park Lane on the site of the older one, once the property of the Earls of Dorchester but more recently owned by the notorious Marquess of Hertford who had died there in 1842. An amateur architect himself, Holford had followed closely the building of this massive new Dorchester House in the style of an ornate Italian Renaissance *palazzo*. Begun in 1851, it was not finally completed until 1863 and though much of the interior decoration in which Coutts took some part belongs to a slightly later period, May and her husband moved in in 1856.

A handsome trousseau was to be chosen in Paris by Anne and May. Writing to her husband in June from the Hotel Castiglione, Anne was tormented by keeping down expenses while May, who, judging by Minnie's intervention at the time of Lord John's marriage proposal, seems to have had a keen eye where money was concerned, was distressed that her father had not seen the marriage settlements nor had had a voice regarding them. There was some hesitation on Anne's part whether it was necessary for James to add two hundred pounds a year to Holford's enormous fortune when he could ill afford it. Coutts had said it was not always done – besides, after James's death it would fall on Coutts to do so and it would be even harder for him. It was neither want of love for May, nor greediness for themselves, that prompted Anne to reflect that with such rich sisters Coutts and Bob would feel the difference of their positions and it was for their parents to look after their sons' future financial prospects. (Or, as Coutts so cogently put it, after his father's death the following year, when debts and demands on the estate were to be met: 'When everybody is helped there will not be much pudding left in the dish.')

Coutts left for Rome soon after the August wedding and spent much of the following year in Italy. Letters were not arriving regularly at Balcarres; when he did write it was to extol the hospitality and virtues of Mr and Mrs Sartoris, a name to conjure with in the artistic world of Rome. Adelaide Sartoris had given up her career as a professional singer in 1842 when at the age of twenty-eight she had married Edward Sartoris, an amateur painter. Hers was a dominating presence in every sense; a daughter of the actor Charles Kemble and, as such, a niece of Sarah Siddons, she had learned to hold an audience, as indeed had her actress sister, Fanny Kemble. Powerfully built and stately in a brocade dress, with the family's aquiline nose, she was not unlike a painting by Tintoretto, and though alarming to Annie Thackeray when a child, she had the engaging quality of enhancing her own parties with the warmth of her reception; yet at the same time, a creature of strong likes and dislikes, she was able to keep at bay those who had no talent or interest to offer.

The company at her musical evenings consisted mostly of painters, sculptors, and those from the literary world. Thackeray had been a regular guest the year before, while the Brownings, and Robert in particular, had gone into society for almost the first time since marriage, finding congenial friends in the Sartoris house. The young painter Frederic Leighton, soon to spring into fame with his painting *Cimabue's Madonna*, was the most intimate and most devoted of the circle. For Mrs Sartoris he entertained the liveliest affection. He was at her house daily and she is ever-present in his letters to his mother in Bath.

Coutts was never an habitué there as was Leighton, but he derived pleasure from the frequent evenings he spent among artists with whom he was in sympathy, a very different group from those who assembled at the Caffè Greco in the Via Condotti: for he had never seen 'a set of more slovenly lounging idlers, enveloped in smoke or talking folly'. At Adelaide Sartoris's, matters were differently managed. The house was open three times a week, or every evening if one felt inclined; there was generally music and one could do there as one liked. Her husband was working at an enormous composition which 'is as likely to be finished as Penelope's webb', and she herself, though singing magnificently, 'makes during the performance a pantomime of the most distorted character, very interesting to an anatomist of expression but a bad accompaniment to music'.

Leighton's mother was uneasy at her son's preoccupation with Mrs Sartoris. Anne Lindsay shared her apprehension: 'The society you describe as belonging to Mrs Sartoris does not appear to me wholesome or desirable. It's like some kind of rich food, you think it good but you feel sick after it

– more like onions.' Coutts did not trouble to argue and as his letters became less frequent Anne wrote: 'I know nothing in the world about you and sometimes I think you dont care to hear about us.' She begged for a pen-and-ink drawing for her screen. 'Do me that kindness, it would only be a little evening's amusement', and he sent her two drawings which she considered as good as Leitch. With her youngest son at the Crimea, her two daughters married and James far from well, her dependence on Coutts, perhaps the most cherished of her children, was touchingly increased. She tried to urge him to come home so that they could have a comfortable talk about plans: she needed the comfort of his support in the wear and tear of each day's reports of the war. But with these anxieties came the stirring news of Bob's heroism at the Battle of the Alma and the family was gravely proud of the young man's gallantry. As senior subaltern he had carried the Queen's colours shot through in a dozen places and the colour staff cut in two, but had with outstanding bravery marched up the slope and planted the standard on the Russian redoubt.

Coutts remained in Italy. He was thirty years old and independent. He was painting in oils and once having fairly made the experiment he would consider whether he was wise to continue in that medium. Besides, by residing abroad he had taken the decisive step of breaking with Lizzie Chambers. Their second child, Coutts Lindsay Chambers, had been born at the end of 1854. By March of the following year Lizzie was being apprised of 'the futility of her hopes which she is still cherishing', namely that Coutts would marry her.

Miss Susannah Henderson, a worthy and God-fearing woman, living in Argyle Cottage, St Leonards, Sheen, with Lizzie in lodgings nearby, was the intermediary for James who was responsible for the bills. How Miss Henderson had been recruited as a go-between is not known – possibly Mr Boyd's help had been requisitioned once again. She did what duty urged her, visited Lizzie, read aloud portions of the scriptures, spoke pious thoughts, had Lizzie in tears, failed to get her to the annual treat of the Sunday scholars with a free entrance ticket, was responsible for the sacking of Lizzie's 'pert, giddy little maid', but had to own to great fears that Lizzie would 'live upon her beauty', rather than honest livelihood. Here Lizzie Chambers slides into the shadows with this second son who was later sent off to Australia, that vast and conveniently distant continent so popular in Victorian times for 'starting a new life'. He too grew to be an artist and in 1890 would exhibit his painting, *Porth, Cornwall*, at the Grosvenor, giving his address as the Garrick Club. Many years on, living in Cyril Mansions, Prince of Wales Road, Battersea, shortly before the First World War and after his father's death, he held an exhibition of his work at the Burlington Gallery, Green Street, Leicester Square, a gallery which aimed at 'becoming the centre for the display of the best modern painting without prejudice to school or styles and with a stern determination to be free from all cliques'.

Coutts was restive. He had a longing to 'pack my traps and be off to the Crimea'. All his friends were there and he felt a kind of deserter. Had he not had a positive and serious object in painting he would have been there long ago. Anne thought he was unhappy and discontented and did not know what to do with himself. She would have preferred an active life for him rather than disposing of his time among wickedness and temptations with 'Leighton and the others'. Anything, she thought, would be better than spending his time 'with a pack of effeminate artists'.

15

Service in the Italian Legion

Coutts had determined to see service in the Crimea with his brother but wanted no well-meant family intervention. He could write lovingly to his mother but he had no intention of sharing his life with her. In the late summer of 1855 he was in England and had been offered and had accepted an invitation to serve as an officer in the Italian Legion. Cavour, the Italian statesman, wished for his own self-serving political reasons to give military help to the Allies in the Crimea. Soldiers were available though undisciplined. Two regiments were formed within the Legion and capable foreign officers were invited to serve. This suited Coutts admirably. His parents were travelling to Florence and had got as far as Genoa. Coutts at headquarters in Turin had received, as colonel, the command of the Lombard Regiment, six hundred strong with recruitment going ahead so rapidly that in another couple of months he would expect to have a thousand. This would complete his roll and by the end of February he hoped they would have a brigade ready for the Crimea. He would shortly be going to Novara, also in Piedmont, where in 1849 heavy fighting had taken place in the Austro-Italian war, and where his men were now quartered. There was a good deal of rebellion amongst them: officers, non-commissioned officers and men had but lately been brought together, some of the men having served in the Sardinian service and some in the Austrian. Until lately the officers had been unknown to one another. Jealousies and insubordination were rife and Coutts was anxious to get to Novara; the first grave offender he could lay hands on, he would make an example of.

All this he had written to his parents on 25 November. Ten days later his father was dead. Both daughters had hurried to Genoa where Coutts joined them. Within a short time Anne continued to Florence with Minnie and May while Coutts, now the head of the family and the heir to Balcarres, took charge of the coffin, carrying it to Scotland for interment.

From Grosvenor Square he wrote to his mother the terms of his father's will and took notes of debts and other business. On receipt of a letter to Anne from Mr Lightbody regarding the settlement of the tuition fee of £10.12s.1d for Master George Chambers, which, he told her, 'General Lindsay was always very prompt at settling', Anne was surprised that steps had not been taken earlier to apprentice the boy. This should be done immediately she told Coutts, adding the stern recommendation 'as a protégé of your father's. A late apprenticeship is a bad thing.' He had shown little wish to discuss the matter and all his mother could discover was that he had talked over the matter with Mr Boyd, who had agreed to keep the boy under his eye as much as possible. He, the elder of Lizzie's offspring, disappears from view until 1871, when as George Coutts Lindsay he re-emerges in Bath Street, Poplar, where having followed his father's artistic steps, he styles himself 'painter'. His neighbours in Poplar were shipwrights and shipbuilders to a man and it seems likely that he was a painter of boats.

Bob was given leave to join his mother in Florence where his sisters had helped to comfort her during her first months of widowhood, but *Wuthering Heights*, strongly recommended by Coutts and read aloud by Minnie, proved anything but a solace; they found it detestable and were unable to continue with it, and indeed it seems hardly a prescription to hand Anne as a restorative.

Coutts, too involved, and whose whole energies were directed towards the Legion, took command of his regiment at Novara in 1856. A finer-looking body of troops he had never seen in the line, though they were as 'complete a set of *condottiere*' as one could imagine. Enlisting at the rate of fifty or sixty a day, many had served in Turkey, Portugal, Sicily, North and South America, Hungary, India or Algiers. But there were difficulties in that those duties generally transacted by the adjutant or sergeant-major in an English regiment were done here by the commanding officer and in the Italian language – though Coutts spoke it with ease, technical terms eluded him.

In late February an incident of some seriousness had been quelled not only by Coutts's firm leadership but, partly too, by that undeniable power to charm which he could exert and which throughout a life of uncertain triumphs and a measure of adversities was an irresistible influence. In this instance an extensive conspiracy in which about five hundred men were implicated had been reported to Coutts by a spy. Officers were to have been shot and the disaffected troops had taken an oath in the plot to march on the Austrian frontier and raise the tricolour. Having communicated with Sir James Hudson, the English envoy at Turin, Coutts closed the barracks, called the officers together, informed them of the affair, telling them that he relied implicitly on their honour. The next morning he had contrived to arrest the two dozen men heading the conspiracy without the bulk of the regiment being aware. He had marched the arrested men to the Novara prison while the regiment had been marched to its drill ground outside the city, still ignorant of the arrests. There Coutts joined them. Finding them in square, he told them what had occurred and what he expected from them as soldiers and men of honour. He then marched them back to barracks and had their dinners served.

Coutts must have made a handsome and commanding figure in his Guards uniform, absolutely at ease with his men, accustomed to a tradition of regimental discipline, and knowing how to enforce it with authority. His men had respected and even admired him, for the next day they had cheered him in barracks until he silenced them on the grounds that soldiers were transgressing their duty when they cheered their commanding officer. Upon which they had been eager to cheer again.

Orders were now given for Coutts to embark his regiment on *Great Britain* and to sail from Genoa to Malta in early March. He assured his mother that if she were unwell and felt alone – Bob having executed a magnificent drawing of a butterfly for the screen had departed for the Crimea – he would throw up his command and join her in Florence at the Villino Borghese, Borgo Pinto.

General Pennefather was in command of the forces in Malta and Coutts received compliments for himself and his regiment. When brigaded with the East Kent and 51st Regiment in review, with 5,000 men on the ground, difficulty arose in the difference of the Italian drill and word of command in manoeuvring with English regiments. His men had behaved admirably – which was more than could be said of the officers. Coutts had half of them under arrest.

With Easter approaching, Anne's thoughts inclined towards her son's spiritual welfare, hoping that there was a good English church in Malta or else he would have very little comfort from the beautiful services of Holy Week 'which the RCs have managed to make so babyish and absurd'. Reading of Coutts's military duties which 'must demand every effort of soul and body', she earnestly hoped that he might be able to do some 'good work for Him, while you are working for your country', so that all his efforts be hallowed and ennobled 'by being dedicated to Him for Christ's sake'.

Nine days later Coutts had left the Italian Legion. He afterwards explained that Burnaby, a long way junior to him in the Army, was in command and had made himself most disagreeable. He had also heard privately that Lord

Clarendon, then Foreign Secretary, had decided that the Legion was to be broken up immediately.

On his way back to England he had stopped at Paris and had seen Ary Scheffer, and with Lords Gifford and Dufferin had shared a lodging in close proximity to the sisters Lady Dufferin and Caroline Norton. Lady Cowley, the wife of the Ambassador, had given a great ball; the night had been lovely and the air warm and Coutts had seldom seen anything prettier or in better taste than the Embassy gardens lighted with coloured lamps, with a large tent erected in the middle.

16
Emancipation

Coutts had enjoyed his four months of military life but the allurements of home were strong. May and June were spent in London; the Somerses, by then an integral part of his life, were sharing July with him at Balcarres where he was now the master. To his mother he described Virginia Somers as a very sweet and lovely person and the most charming woman in England, to which Anne took an amused exception, begging him to remember that Minnie and May would run her hard.

Anne was at Westonbirt with the Holfords and wanted a small pen and ink drawing from Lord Somers. 'You know the screen is my hobby, you must let me ride it and help me to feed it.' And from Dorchester House where Leitch had dined with them, she wrote of the Rembrandt etchings, of the drawings and prints unnumbered and extremely interesting, but she felt that for one person only to own such treasures was a pity, 'for they kill each other. No one has time to enjoy them.'

Throughout those months that Coutts was in England his mother and sisters were on the look-out for a suitably rich marriage. He was thirty-two, it was time he settled down and had an heir. Money and background were all-important. He was partly willing and would act quickly if he could find a likely girl. There was talk of one of the Percys though Lord Lindsay was heard to say that he hoped his brother-in-law did not suppose that '*veni vidi vince*' was to be his motto in the field of Cupid 'unless the challenged party surrendered at discretion'. He did not think a Percy would easily succumb but begged that his remarks should not be repeated to Coutts as he might not relish Lindsay's levity. Another name put forward by Coutts was that of Mrs Domville. Isabella Maria, daughter of Sir George Arthur, Bt, had married in 1842 Compton Charles Domville who had died ten years later in Nice. As the son of Sir Compton Domville, Bt and of Elizabeth, daughter of Charles Lindsay, Hon. and Right Revd Bishop of Kildare, he had made the alliance a cousinly one, but Anne was on her guard. Of her true worth and high principles there could be no doubt; her conduct towards her husband during his prolonged illness had been sweet and affectionate. She would be a kind daughter-in-law and a winning sister, but she was probably older than Coutts and as she had had no children perhaps she might not now. Of her looks of course Coutts could judge: pretty and pleasing certainly but with no charm of conversation and, as a finishing stroke, Anne fancied her rather dull. Also the financial aspect was tricky. A large income from the Domvilles for her life, to cease at death, and what she might have to bequeath was not known. But besides these disadvantages so carefully enumerated, Anne feared – and rightly (though partly of her own doing) – that Coutts had worked himself up to a frame of mind where marriage was imperative but where his heart was unsatisfied. To sacrifice the sort of liberty very dear to him for love and affection would cost him nothing, but without them he would be haunted with remembrances of travels that could no longer be undertaken. Poor Mrs Domville. The grounds for her emergence on the matrimonial stage were as transient as they were unlikely and Coutts was already hatching a plan to spend the whole of next year abroad in the company of the Somerses.

He had not yet revealed this to his mother when he joined her at Grosvenor Square in the autumn and she, who loved him so deeply, was no longer at ease with him. In a very frank letter to Minnie – and it must have cost her severely to speak as she did – she wrote:

He is very kind and affectionate in manner but he keeps me in a constant terror. He is so different from us all. So liberal-minded – so full of progress – looks down upon us *all* as old-fashioned, prejudiced, narrow-minded people who cannot keep up with the necessities of the age. He is so fluent and clever that you always – however you may know you are in the right – find yourself in five minutes quite in the wrong box. He has a most kind heart and I verily believe would do anything I asked him to do as a kindness – believing me at the same time to be a prejudiced old woman for wishing it. He thinks all the family terribly antiquated in their ideas. If he were not my son I should think him quite delightful. In theory he has the utmost contempt for money but I think he would probably spend a good deal. In short as I said before he frightens me and since he arrived I have been in a state of extreme nervous *tension* and more than ever longing to be with you.

An old story, repeated in all forms and in all ages, and Coutts, unfettered and far more worldly than his family, with his youth, his name, his many attractions, was determined not to conform but to make his own life in the company of his chosen friends – and with his inherited money. The year 1857 was to be spent partly in Rome with the Somerses as his companions and partly in *Falcon*, the yacht he would be sharing with them in a sketching expedition to the Greek islands.

On the morning of the above letter he had gone off to Southampton to meet Lord Somers on some business, 'of course not to be divulged' to his mother. He had told her he had been thoroughly appreciated by his cousins who took his advice in everything but it was a provocation to her that everyone should spoil him, as it gave him an inflated opinion of himself and his powers.

By December he was arranging the yacht transactions before the Somerses left for Italy. Their share would be £750 and he himself would see about getting Virginia Somers a horse as she would not have a chance of purchasing a good one in Rome. His groom could take it with his own two horses via Marseilles and Coutts would be following soon after. With a letter of introduction to Ary Scheffer whom they would see as they went through Paris, he wished them a good journey while fearing it would be bitterly cold. On 10 January he too was on his way. In retrospect 1857 was probably the most enjoyable of his thirty-five years.

He was soon comfortably established close to the Trinità dei Monti in the Tempietto, the house which stood at the angle of the two streets, Via Sistina and Gregoriana, and was said to have been once inhabited by Claude Lorrain. The Somerses had their apartments on the first floor, Coutts on the third. His sitting-room looked out over all Rome and to add to his good fortune he was able to secure a large studio in the house opposite with a good light. Adjoining the Tempietto was the house where Federigo Zuccaro was once occupant of the ground floor while above, in one of the first-floor rooms, were frescoes by Overbeck, Cornelius and others of the 'Nazarene' group, commissioned by the Prussian consul, Bartoldy.

Coutts's days were now idyllically spent. In the mornings he worked diligently at his painting and had in hand a composition of a child and *contadina* who was old and ugly (and here he had not been able to resist gently teasing his mother), not wishing to 'have any beauty to distract him'. Poor reassurance for Anne, aware of two young illegitimate boys and the disreputably entrancing Lizzie.

He lunched with the Somerses (they were all great luncheon eaters), after which he rode out with Lord Somers. They were both skilled photographers, in advance of their day, as many of Coutts's salt prints taken at this time show. They would dine together unless he dined out – Rome afforded many friends, among whom the widowed Lady Marian Alford, sister of the third Marquess of North-ampton, figured prominently. Her youth had been spent largely in Italy, her income was a handsome one, her enthusiasm for 'art' was generally acknowledged; she was worldly, she was extravagant, and her position in society assured. She was all but reverential to the prominent artistic and literary personages in Rome and Coutts on his first introduction found her artificial with a desire to appear clever (an attribute which Elizabeth Barrett Browning had noted as 'affectation'), but he found she improved vastly on acquaintance and came to like her extremely. Who can say that she did not flatter him, for before long he was writing home that he had been persuaded by Lady Marian to go to a fancy dress ball as Vandyck in a black velvet costume with lace collar and sleeves, loose 'britches' and black silk stockings and, 'it will amuse you to hear', he continued, 'that I have lately become a Beauty. People have taken it into their heads to fancy me very good-looking. This is very ridiculous for I am certainly no better looking than I used to be, this quite between you and me.'

Before leaving London he had sent to friends copies of his new, privately published tragedy, *Boadicea*, and enthusiastic letters of congratulation reached him in Rome.[14] Perhaps he had hoped that by sending copies to the actor-managers Alfred Wigan at the Olympic Theatre and Charles Kean at the Princess he might hope to see his play performed on the stage. But Wigan retired from management within a few months and Charles Kean announced his farewell season the next year, so the author's hopes never materialized. But the great piece of news from home was that Bob was gazetted to the Victoria Cross for his gallantry both at the Battle of the Alma and on the Inkerman Heights.

News of one kind or another was sent to Haigh where Anne was staying: the Empress of Russia was expected and had engaged thirty carriages and everything in proportion; the Somerses had sent for their children to spend a few weeks; and, to electrify his mother, he had 'met a very pretty and graceful girl of the name of Duncombe', a relation and great friend of Lady Marian Alford, her mother dead, a resemblance to his sister May in figure and manner – and, to the point, that she would have £5,000 a year from her grandfather. Her father was in bad health. Coutts had met her only twice but had liked extremely what he had seen. Virginia Somers had been much taken with her and had invited her to Albano where they were all staying to avoid the Roman sirocco. 'I dont suppose there is anything in this,' Coutts continued, 'nevertheless I know you like to hear whatever passes through my mind on such matters.' Perhaps unfortunately their letters had crossed and Anne had written a shade reprovingly of May (whom Miss Duncombe was said to resemble) 'looking very handsome but she wears great crinoline petticoats and instead of a poetical creation looks like a beautiful well-dressed woman'. Soon Anne wrote again: 'I cannot find in the peerage what Miss Duncombe she is. Is she really good and amiable and true hearted? After all darling, this is the bread. The butter is the other things.'

No further word comes from his pen though Anne in some anxiety wrote of her great wish for his next letter and to hear something of Miss Duncombe's visit to Albano. 'I think everything makes me anxious and nervous now, my happiness lies so much out of myself and in other people. Dont forget me and always love me, dearest Coutts.'

17

Mount Athos

As late spring merged into summer, preparations for a cruise through the Greek islands were under way. Coutts's horses were to be sent home, so too the Somerses' children after a few weeks with their parents. Virginia was an obsessive mother; adoring her little girls she was nevertheless so exacting in their upbringing that nurses and nursery governesses came and went with clockwork regularity; the children were now on their seventh governess in five years.

Writing from Malta to tell his mother of a Maltese lace mantilla he was sending her, he casually let fall that Virginia's sister, Mrs Prinsep, would be delivering it at Grosvenor Square and he hoped that some afternoon she would drive out to Little Holland House where G. F. Watts was being cherished by the Prinseps, and make her acquaintance. Coutts thought she would like Sara Prinsep (which seems unlikely given the persistent lionizing and the reputation of what was loosely known as Bohemian society to be encountered there) and would be interested in seeing Watts's drawings. The gardens, too, would please her excessively.

It was here that members of the Pre-Raphaelite Brotherhood would gather to enjoy strawberries under the trees in season in the companionship of an admired 'stunner', and play croquet on the lawn. Musicians, actresses and singers were welcomed and worshipped and over it all hung a suggestion of laxity of morals and a general freedom of behaviour. Coutts was quite at home here, so too were Thackeray, Burne-Jones, Tennyson, Rossetti and the whole tribe of Pattle sisters: Julia Cameron with her camera,

Virginia Somers with her charm and distinction. Watts had
not yet married Ellen Terry, but Louisa Herbert, the actress
from the Olympic Theatre and a model of Rossetti, who
was 'under the protection' of two rich lovers, would sit to
the young artists while they made studies of her. The
flirtatious Georgina Treherne, admired by Watts, was there
when not in the throes of some absorbing romance or
advancing her career as an amateur singer engaged for a
concert at a private house.

The next six months were spent by Coutts and the
Somerses and their crew sailing the Aegean Sea. Coutts's
first glimpse of Greece an hour after dusk was of rugged and
distant hills wrapped in uncertain vapour, glimmering
between sea and heaven under a rising moon. The islands of
Hydra and Aegina as he passed them the next morning
appeared to him an evocation of the west coast of Scotland,
but the new Athens of 1857, mostly built by German
architects, earned his contempt for its 'exquisite bad taste'.
Only the Acropolis, isolated on its rock, seemed to breathe
an art and feeling which no book could revive. A Venetian
tower at one corner had assumed, chameleon-like, the
colour and quality of things around it. Nothing of the
present day intruded and Coutts could reflect that there,
had ruin advanced her step by two thousand years,
Demosthenes might have sat and mourned the physical, as
he had the moral, ruin of his city.

Across the sea to Mytilene and then a leisurely progress
up the Turkish coast occupied the next weeks, through the
Dardanelles and the Sea of Marmara to Constantinople
where Anne had hoped he might acquire additions for the
'tableau chest' at Balcarres for there were 'such beautiful
queer Paolo Veronese looking things to be had there'. In
future years when Blanche Lindsay, Coutts's wife, would
entertain Prince Leopold and Sir Arthur Sullivan with
charades, it was this tableau chest which was dredged for
appropriate clothing, but Coutts mentioned no purchases

of that kind other than a beautiful Persian shawl for Anne for which she thanked him with loving trust. 'I wonder when you bought it – what I was doing at the time, that the wish to give me pleasure was in your heart. I hope I was thinking of you then, it is very likely for your image is often with me.'

Coutts was a faithless correspondent and Anne was hard put to it to know where to reach him with an account of Bob's award of the Victoria Cross. 'The sight was as beautiful as sight could be,' she wrote. She and her two daughters and Lindsay had been placed just behind the Queen. Bob had looked particularly handsome with his great height and distinguished bearing. How proud the three women must have been and one wonders a little what Coutts may have experienced as he read his mother's account. The Queen had smiled as she had pinned on the cross and had said a few words but Bob had been unable to catch them.

Hopes of the yachting party visiting the Crimea had been dashed when it had become evident that the Russians would have put every kind of impediment in their way. A week camping out on a mountain of Brusa was a delightful alternative and silk for dresses was obtained for Minnie and May from the celebrated silk-spinners of the city.

From Mount Athos in September Coutts wrote of the beauty of the forms of the mountains and of the buildings, some of the fifth century, and of the old monk anchorite standing, bent double, at the mouth of his cave which held nothing but dried leaves and a cross; and of the simplicity and kindliness of those monks they had encountered, both to himself and Somers, and to Virginia as well. For Virginia Somers had been as welcome on Mount Athos as the others, as the rules respecting women landing were, according to Coutts, far more lax than they had once been and Virginia had written home of how the monks had taken her one evening over the monastery gardens and had insisted on giving her fruit from every tree as they passed; she had tasted pomegranate, citron and peach. They had lived there in tents for two months, in perfect weather and harmony, and if this was a *ménage à trois* on Mount Athos it must surely stand as the only one of its kind. Innumerable sketches had been made since they had cast anchor in early June and from Mount Athos many more would follow.

Coutts's letters were mainly descriptive and from these his family could not have known – any more than we as onlookers can judge now – the moods and perceptions, the subtle repressions or evasions undergone by the three participants in this human comedy. No echoes or reflections seemed to disturb the cloudless golden days spent lazily on the Aegean Sea, under the spell of the calm surface of the waters; yet not one of the three would have been insensible to the shared romance of place and circumstance, perhaps awakening a responsiveness only partly concealed.

A final call at Smyrna and the long sunlit days of sailing would be over. Sunset, twilight, and the starry nights would soon be exchanged for Grosvenor Square, London. But Coutts would not exert himself. Virginia and her maid were going home from Marseilles to fetch the children and bring them back to Rome while he and Somers would sail by steamer from Malta to Civita Vecchia, have a week in Naples, a few days in Rome, and 'Thus my dearest Mum,' he wrote on 4 November, 'I shall be later in England than I had proposed', and hoped to be there by early December. He had plans for her to accompany him back to Rome for he intended to return there in January. The Somerses would be in the Tempietto, he at the Casa Zuccaro next door, and Lady Marian Alford on the floor beneath his. If, however, she preferred, she could join Lady Somers directly as she was about to return to Italy. This had been Virginia's proposition, he had said. Meanwhile the gaps between Coutts's letters had given Anne to think she would never hear from him again. It was six weeks since his last. 'I believe he has settled in Smyrna and got a hareem and a chibouk,'* she had written to May. At Dunecht when at last she heard from him, she was bound to refuse the tempting suggestion of an Italian winter. Had it not been for the dreadful uprooting and numerous domestic difficulties, and more especially the cold journey at that season of the year, how much she would have enjoyed spending the winter with Coutts – 'I long to see you my darling.'

Virginia was to be in London that week so she would miss her but Anne was delighted with her letters: 'There is something suave and harmonious about her.' Then Coutts had gone down with influenza in Rome and she wondered when she would see him or whether he would be wandering away somewhere with the Somerses for it was now Christmas. Having given up all hope of him, she was at Haigh with Lord Balcarres (now a widower) and the Lindsays. One last word to Coutts closed the year 1857. She had opened by mistake a letter enclosed in a letter to her and she had not looked at the direction which on inspection she saw was addressed to Coutts. But she had seen the signature in time to prevent her reading it. The letter had been from Lizzie Chambers. Lizzie had evidently fallen on her feet – or gone to the dogs, in vulgar parlance and Lindsay estimate – and had found a well-to-do protector, for at the opera one evening Bob had seen her in a box in the tier above the Holford box, and very handsomely dressed she was too. 'I fear this does not speak well for her, poor thing.' Lizzie with a final flourish of fine feathers bows out of the story.

Coutts was nursing his influenza in Rome after a second attack while Lady Marian Alford was applying mustard poultices to his neck 'in the most grandmotherly manner', he circumspectly told Anne, but his failing to return home was a disappointment to her, especially as the marble

* A long Turkish pipe.

monument to his father for the chapel at Balcarres had arrived from Italy after four months at sea. The ship had sprung a leak and had had to put in at a Spanish port where it had been unladen, but Francis McCracken of the Belfast shipping firm and an early patron of Rossetti had examined the marble on arrival and had found no harm done. And though Coutts wrote in February that he had nothing to keep him in Rome except the wish to finish his oil painting of *Romeo and Juliet* and that unless he could accomplish a very good picture – and one that would be acknowledged as such – he might be tempted to consider painting as a pastime and nothing more; yet it was June before he left Italy. One senses an apprehension on his mother's part; a model was more or less synonymous with a mistress and she thought a model for Juliet might have a 'Southern character, yet the Northern mysterious sweetness and purity would still hang about her – a beautiful mingling of both'.

The Somerses were always in the forefront of his letters: the children were pretty, particularly the eldest, Isabel; the Queen of Spain's fancy dress ball for which he had superintended Virginia's dress had been a four days' occupation and much more trouble than to introduce and carry a bill as every article of dress had been a battlefield. In April, from Albano, there were definite plans for another expedition by yacht, again in company of the Somerses, with a return home by himself through the Tyrol, but further delay followed. In June, and with the Somerses, Coutts was held up at the hospice at Andermatt on the St Gotthard by Virginia having been seized with a fever after a very hot journey through Italy. They were detained there a week, with neither physician nor maid. Coutts doctored her with Hercy's domestic medicine and a homeopathic box of tinctures, bringing down her pulse after three days. During this time they were most uneasy and had sat up all night. 'They all have queer ways,' Anne thought. But at least Coutts would be home in a week.

Within a day or so of this letter, on stepping out of his carriage at the hospice on his way south to Bellinzona, the first person John Ruskin had seen was Virginia Somers and presently afterwards 'Lord Somers in a straw hat; smoking', with whom of course he had been associated at Oxford. He had spent the evening with them 'very pleasantly'; no mention of Coutts nor of Virginia's illness. Perhaps both were concealed from him; Lord Somers particularly did not wish his wife's illness to be known, nor perhaps that the third member of the party was Coutts. The next morning, 12 June, Ruskin reported to his father that Virginia had run down to the house door herself and had asked him to breakfast with them, but its being a beautiful and cloudless morning he had preferred a walk; besides, he knew they were just leaving, with a long day's journey ahead and would be tired.[15]

Hopes for Coutts's return were shipwrecked again. Virginia Somers had written from the Hotel Mirabeau in Paris on 19 June on Coutts's behalf to tell his mother that they were detained in Paris because of his 'feverish attack' but that Dr Gastier, president of the Homeopathic Society had promised a recovery in two or three days. On 24 June Coutts arrived in Grosvenor Square, brown, very thin, but well, his hair touched with grey, but abundant and silky. To his mother's delight he was affectionate, happy, glad to be with her and much more like his old self than when he was last home. He had with him a portfolio of watercolour landscapes and a beautiful head of Virginia 'in material like fresco'. Lord Lindsay was full of admiration and thought Coutts now competent to take his place among professionals; the composition of *Romeo and Juliet* promised to be very fine and 'the beautiful portrait of Lady Somers, herself a most beautiful woman, has excited great admiration', and Lord Balcarres trusted Coutts would turn out a fine painter, not as a portrait painter 'for that is low in the scale of art and has numerous rivals'. In the last days of June Coutts was

launched in a world of dissipation; Anne would see him in
the mornings and would have a long comfortable talk, after
which he would evaporate and she would hear no more of
him. He was happy and pleased with himself and other
people. And Anne, though fully aware of the blessings
which surrounded her, told Minnie that she was so low and
out of spirits that she could not keep the tears out of her eyes
for five minutes together.

Bob, however, was giving her much happiness. The
Prince of Wales at the age of seventeen had appointed him
an equerry, while at the same time Bob was making the most
desirable marriage. Harriet, the bride-to-be, was the daughter of Samuel Loyd, first Baron Overstone, banker and
financier of high reputation. As an only child and heiress to
a great fortune, her parents were reluctant to entrust her to a
young man until they were very sure of his uprightness and
worth. With Bob they would have no misgivings. Coutts
being the head of the family had had the duty of informing
himself of Lord Overstone's financial proposals, and these
had been so liberal that they made Bob independent of his
wife. The name of Loyd was to be harnessed to that of
Lindsay and the Overstones' Berkshire estates of Lockinge,
near Wantage, were settled on him for life. Harriet Loyd
was the ideal match for Bob and was warmly welcomed into
the family while Coutts, more than ever aware that he
should emulate his brother, had embarked once again on a
yachting expedition with the Somerses. This had taken him
to Tangier but he was in Scotland at Rose Hall, the
Holfords' shooting box, in Ross-shire, by the end of August
and shortly after at Balcarres to welcome the Somerses and
a host of friends.

He was sitting to Watts now for the head of Edward I in
the Lincoln's Inn fresco of *Justice: A Hemicycle of
Lawgivers*, in competition with Virginia Somers whose
head, if not her limbs, is probably depicted in one or other of
the nine large frescoes of *The Elements* painted for the walls

of the Somerses' house, 7 Carlton House Terrace, and again in *Apollo and Diana* with her bow.

At Balcarres Coutts was being badgered for more work for the family screen. Away from his friends he was 'rather sick of the country', as he told Lord Somers, 'and have taken to cut down trees in desperation and to have photographs done of the family including the servants. Dont that sound like a man on his last legs for something to do?' Inviting himself to Eastnor Castle he closed his jeremiad: 'That d — d screen has been the bane of my life'.

Autumn ended on a more cheerful note though December closed gloomily enough. Anne noted that Coutts, who had been in London following his visit to Eastnor, had been re-called there 'by telegraph' as Virginia, the youngest child, was ill. She thought it 'a great misfortune' to be so depend-ent on another person, but so far it was lucky that the husband and wife were of the same mind on the subject. The child recovered and Anne was invited down to join them. This was her first visit to the castle and she found the house full of tapestries, carved wood and an amount of beautiful curiosities assembled by Lord Somers and picked up in different countries; also about forty entire suits of armour. But though the park was very fine and for a considerable distance the yews on either side of a long drive were of a vast size,[17] she could not but find it 'a bad, uncomfortable scrambly rambly cold house', full of people on this occasion. Coutts remained until the New Year enjoying himself enormously, being made much of by everyone. Lord Somers could do nothing without him and he ruled Virginia and the children. It was a constant 'Where's Coutts?', from morning to night.

He was barely back in London when a sudden summons reached him from Eastnor begging him to return as the little girl had contracted diphtheria. Having 'a turn for doctoring', he got full instructions from his own doctor and went down by the express train. A specialist had been sent for too late to avert the tragedy. The young Virginia had died in Coutts's arms. In attending on her, a good deal of poison was said to have settled in his throat without assuming the form of diphtheria, and though the nurse had caught it and had been in severe danger, Coutts quickly recovered and joined his mother at Balcarres at the end of January 1859, but having shared in their deep affliction he was drawn still closer to Lord Somers and his wife.

18

Too Many Irons in the Fire

If Anne had been urging matrimony on a reluctant Coutts while he had been successfully evading the issue, Hannah FitzRoy on her part had been bringing up Blanche with no other goal in sight. As with all mothers of that class and generation, an eldest son was to be hoped for, preferably endowed with a handsome fortune. This was logical since young girls were trained for that and for no other future and Blanchy was being very highly trained indeed. Her invalid brother had died in 1858 in their Paris apartment, Avenue Gabriel, and her father, scarcely recovering from so cruel a sorrow, had followed Arthur to the grave the next year. He had been appointed First Commissioner of Works but illness, breakdown, and the development of religious mania had forced him to resign. Death, when it came at 14 Lewes Crescent, Brighton, in December 1859, had left shattered the lives of his wife and daughter. Only that summer he had taken them to Scotland and on their return journey, when crossing the Firth from Bruntisland, Blanche, standing by his side on deck in the twilight with a volume of Scott's poems in her hand, had heard and would remember his saying, as he pointed eastwards towards the coast of Fife, that that was where he would like to put down his roots.

The London house in Upper Grosvenor Street belonged to Hannah and now Blanche, rising sixteen, would go from there to her dancing lessons clad in black wool half covered with mourning crape. Intermittently for close on two years, properly chaperoned, she attended Heatherley's art class in Newman Street, one of the only two private schools of art in London. After FitzRoy's death Hannah Mayer had found it impossible to settle. To Louise, the wife of Hannah's brother, Sir Anthony de Rothschild, Bt, of Aston Clinton, she seemed 'a perfect nilly', but Hannah was in a state of depression and poor health. Dragging her daughter with her, she sought consolation in the most melancholy fashion, journeying along the banks of the Rhine.

It was Constance, the Rothschilds' eldest daughter, who as Blanchy's only friend was the recipient of her first cousin's dispiriting letters from Frankfort, the cradle of the Rothschild family. After so many years of marriage, and furthermore now a widow, Hannah was accepted, once culpable perhaps, but accepted by the Rothschilds nonetheless. New Year was spent in their old house in the Altstadt and Blanche reported that she had drunk Pernod and had been given sleeve studs of lapis lazuli and a brooch to match. She had not much to say of Frankfort other than that she was having riding lessons which were at least a pleasure to look forward to. At Munich which was visited for the Pinakotek the heat and general bustle gave her a headache and she felt limp, and her mother was suffering from weakness – a sad, self-pitying couple. From Schaffhausen Blanche had Lake Constance to complain of: 'I had no idea that the lake which bears your name could be so disagreeable.'[18]

Having nothing to read, since the Tauchnitz editions could be perused in a day, and having familiarized herself with Lord Dover's *Life of Frederick II King of Prussia* (1832), she had no relish for the first volume of Carlyle's great work on the same subject, so she lay on the sofa most of the day making a little mat and threading white beads. At Schwalbach to take the waters, she fed on 'everlasting boiled veal and stewed prunes' and watched the Germans eating with their knives.

While Blanche was gripped in the tediousness of filling uneventful days, Coutts had set up a studio for himself at 11 Grosvenor Square, no longer a house for the whole family since Minnie, Lindsay, and their children had the use of 21 Berkeley Square, at the corner of Bruton Street, once Lady Anne Barnard's and now the family's London home. Bob and his wife were establishing themselves at Lockinge with the advantage of her parents' house in town at Carlton Gardens. May Holford had the splendours of Dorchester House which yielded magnificently to her happy disposition for entertaining, and it was here that Coutts would spend a fair amount of time for several years. His sister had engaged him to embellish in fresco some of the newly-built rooms and to his pleasure in the work was added a healthy degree of acclaim.

One day, bringing with her one of her most constant admirers, Virginia Somers had pointed out to Lord Lansdowne some drawings by Coutts hanging in his studio. Lord Lansdowne had mistakenly believed them to be 'compositions of the great old masters' and wondered where Coutts had found them, thinking that they should be better known. He could scarcely believe it when they were revealed as Coutts's own work. Anne's hopeful assumption that 'I think we shall be proud of Coutts yet' is in painful contrast to the family's early confidence in a distinguished future.

Alive to an overall conception that art should be made applicable to everything and that, like the great Italians, an artist should be architect and sculptor as well as painter, able to turn his hand to anything, Coutts investigated the possibilities of painting on china from his own designs and set about mastering the difficulties. At Stoke-on-Trent, home of Minton's pottery works, he gave his coloured design for a large oval dish to Mr Goode who was said to have been 'transported' with it and hoped Coutts would make more designs for him. This Coutts probably would, stipulating only that the Lindsay crest of a tent should appear in some part of the pattern. The design for the particular plate in question, to be executed in majolica, represented the sea goddess Amphitrite and the Nereids. 'Like a Giulio Romano', Anne thought, 'with a fulness of classical youth, joy and sportiveness that is very rare now.'

Coutts had been surprised to find the Minton works operating on so large a scale, with 1,600 people employed and plates, dishes, tiles, pots, water pots and jam pots produced in hundreds of thousands. He had commented on chamber-pots being a chief source of revenue besides being an 'article of universal application'; in the manufactory itself the workmen used them as dinner pots and he had noticed several very pretty girls feeding out of one of the largest he had ever seen.

Besides this new activity Coutts had formulated a plan whereby the Dilettanti Society and the Arundel Society might cooperate. This last, founded in 1848, largely as a result of Lord Lindsay's *History of Christian Art*, had been set up to preserve for subscribers, by a process of chromolithography, watercolour facsimiles of Italian frescoes and other early paintings. To Anne it had seemed, though probably as the reflection of a remark by Coutts, that the Dilettanti consisted principally of 'rich elderly men who subscribe largely, meet to dine and talk and do little for Art'. The proposal put forward was to join in a scheme for making reduced copies of the Elgin Marbles in order to facilitate their acquisition by artists and others and to promote the study of Greek sculpture. On 7 April Coutts wrote to Mr W. R. Hamilton, the highly esteemed secretary of the Dilettanti, to the effect that he had been commissioned by the Council of the Arundel Society to place this invitation in his hands, adding: 'The name of Hamilton has been so identified with the Elgin Marbles that I need scarcely ask his forgiveness if his own children cause him a little trouble.' The minutes of the Dilettanti Society show an inclination to assist in the matter but the scheme was eventually dropped.[19]

The previous year had seen the death of Ary Scheffer,

the Lindsay family's particular friend under whom Coutts
had studied. He had engaged to write an appreciation of
Scheffer and his performance for the *Quarterly Review*
which ran to forty pages of print. In May he and Mrs
Grote had crossed the Channel together to be present at a
posthumous exhibition of the artist's work. Mrs Grote,
wife of the eminent historian, was sixty-seven years of age,
tall and stately, large blue eyes likened to carriage lamps,
of formidable intellect, a dominating though brilliant
woman 'who, though a blue stocking, habitually wore red
ones and displayed them with as little reticence as she
showed in her conversation'. She was also very proud of
her small feet and wore short dresses to show them off.[20]
May Holford was prodigiously amused at this incon-
gruous couple starting off for Paris together, both of them
distinguished – Mrs Grote for her brilliance of intellect,
Coutts for his artistic skills and charm of manner.

At Balcarres that summer, in the company of Virginia
Somers and her nephew Arthur Prinsep, Coutts was full of
plans for the garden but he could not afford to do much
and for all his enthusiasms – the Dorchester House
cartoons, the Minton works, the joining of the Arundel
Society with the Dilettanti – Anne was anxious that 'Perhaps dear Coutts has too many irons in the fire but I
believe the furnace is hot enough for them all if he will only
take each in turn.' At the end of the year Coutts was
handing out advice at Lockinge for the interior of the
house and settled a line of approach through the park.
Bob's wife, Harriet, hoped that at home at Balcarres
Coutts would take a hand at the screen but there is no
indication that he did so: on the contrary, he had a
shooting party and, 'looking beautiful', had been attending
meetings of the 6th (Volunteer) Battalion of the Black
Watch. The gardeners, the two keepers, and the sawmill
carpenter had enlisted and Coutts was to clothe them.

In the last year or two, meanwhile, Blanche's days had

followed much the same pattern as the earlier ones: six months at Bournemouth with her mother, followed by Switzerland, Munich again, a month at St Leonard's-on-Sea, and off to Brussels, Antwerp, Ghent, Bruges, with interludes in London when she had attended her art classes at Heatherley's. From Nice, in January 1863, she had written to her cousin Constance of busy employment in making useful, ornamental and uncommon objects for a bazaar, quickly made, but fatiguing to the eyes. She was drawing from models, though they were 'utterly unpunctual' and faithless. She had a piano but never practised; was a subscriber to two music libraries and had joined the choir of the English church. Although lovely excursions were to be made, of course she had been nowhere and her teeth ached endlessly. Occasionally she would creep out and take a little drive but was more often at home in dullness. Bulwer-Lytton she watched as he paced up and down the Promenade des Anglais 'clad in a singular manner'; every evening after the *table d'hôte* dinner he would entice a magic circle around him and would terrify them with brilliantly told ghost and table-rapping stories.[21]

From these anaemic communications one might judge the writer to have been a victimized daughter tied to Hannah's apron, without talent or allure. This was not the case. Her mother had always been convinced that 'Blanchy's dazzling beauty' had caused all Continentals to stare her out of countenance on steamers, railroads and hotels and, as Henry FitzRoy had done to Hannah, she had forbidden Blanche to lift up her veil, though to Annie Thackeray she seemed 'neither prettier nor less affected than in former days'. There are clear indications that she had been well grounded in English and French literature, had studied geometry and quadratic equations, her needlework was accomplished with fairy-like perfection, she sang with a sweet voice, was fluent in French and probably in German, drew with precision and ability, and her playing of the violin would develop into something first-rate. All she needed was to be launched into society and after a carefully regulated youth find her feet among her contemporaries while collecting the most august paragon for a husband. Her day had almost come.

19

Preparations for Marriage

The part played by Coutts in the decorative embellishment of Dorchester House is difficult to define as few records appear to have survived. The family wrote of them with lively approbation and G. F. Watts who was engaged at the time in painting murals at Bowood for Lord Lansdowne, and at Carlton House Terrace for the Somerses, praised them highly and offered to join in partnership with him. It was probably through Robert Holford (if not through the Somerses) that Coutts had come to know Watts, for the latter had used a room in Dorchester House for the housing of his large canvases until Mrs Prinsep had swept him off willingly to Little Holland House.

At a time when there was a revival of interest in mural painting both here and abroad, many techniques were being tried. Coutts appears to have evolved a method or medium of his own, the knowledge of which he had shared with his assistant Charles Couzens, miniaturist, copier, and only recently studio assistant to Watts. May Holford was awake to the possibility of Couzens making use of this knowledge and receiving the credit before Coutts had established his name in connection with it. Also, that her brother, unguarded in speech, might divulge the method to Watts without being aware of having done so. No further information emerges regarding the use of Coutts's artistic invention and with the destruction of Dorchester House we remain ignorant of its success.

In printed accounts of this 'private palace of monumental construction', Coutts appears to have been given control of all the decorative work in the house, for much of which he made designs. Many were executed under his direction by Italian artists. Of his own painting he was responsible for a series running beneath the saucer domes of the walls of two of the first-floor arcaded galleries overlooking the magnificent staircase. He was also responsible for a frieze ('a bright bit of work') in the red drawing-room – one of three. For the dining-room Holford commissioned Alfred Stevens to design the doors, furniture and all the fixtures, and it was here that he executed his masterpiece of the great fireplace: two majestic Carrara marble caryatids 'almost Michaelangeloesque in their superb proportions and flowing draperies', supporting a bardiglia marble mantle-piece. A sideboard was also his but work on the Wellington monument in St Paul's Cathedral occupied so much of his time that the room was never completed and his proposed design for the ceiling cove was laid aside. Coutts took this up, not very successfully from all accounts, introducing a flight of birds against an azure sky.[22]

His portrait of his mother was accepted by the Royal Academy for their 1862 Summer Exhibition. *Fraser's Magazine* commented favourably in July on 'his remarkable amateur work evidently based on study of Mr Watts', and that it stood high upon the list of good portraits. It was well placed and acknowledged a success; Anne staying at The Priory, Reigate, with the Somerses, exclaimed that Coutts had become a famous painter and had been besieged with congratulations and admiration. Tom Taylor, dramatist, journalist, and later editor of *Punch*, praised Coutts the following year in the *Fine Arts Quarterly Review* as 'the distinguished representative of high art as practised by non-professional painters'.

He still showed no real inclination towards matrimony although there had been soundings early in the year (1863) when Coutts and Minnie had stayed at Eastnor Castle and he had been rather pressed into an 'understanding' with Lady Adelaide Talbot, a devoted niece by marriage of his widowed cousin Louisa Waterford. She answered the first requirement, that of patrician birth, since her father, the 18th Earl of Shrewsbury, had married the sister of the 'wild Marquess' of Waterford whom Louisa had mourned for the last four years. However, she had inherited an unfortunate legacy of 'untamed ancestry', negligible in herself though more accentuated in her sisters, the Ladies Pembroke and Lothian, and this had made the match not altogether desirable. 'As features go,' commented the irrepressible Walburga Lady Paget, 'Lady Adelaide was perhaps the handsomest woman in England', with 'large lustrous eyes and rose-leaf complexion', and seen at the Queen's ball in white satin covered with fresh Cape jasmine and diamonds she was superb. Although charmless and speaking in a high monotonous falsetto, and with a bad carriage, she was nevertheless 'the salt of the earth.'[23] Coutts, who at the outset had seemed responsive, now wavered, much to Anne's relief who hoped Virginia would not persist and in particular would talk as little as possible to him about marriage 'for I think all these attempts do harm to him and keep up a nervous state of mind'. From what was to follow it is certain that Virginia wanted a hand in the matrimonial stakes: a wife for Coutts of her own choosing, young and subdued, forever grateful to the (scheming) hand which had engineered the introduction. With praise for Virginia from May and Coutts ringing in her ears, Anne had never tumbled to the manoeuvring being conducted to ensure a pliable wife. It may well have been the result of May Holford's constantly urging her brother to take this forward step in marriage which occasioned Somers to tell his wife in the autumn that he and Coutts had left Rose Hall for Dunecht to Coutts's intense satisfaction. He had never seen him so fidgety and miserable as he was with the Holfords. It was of no benefit for him to go there and by the time he had reached Balcarres in October he was better 'both in mind and body'. Louisa Waterford was most probably a guest at the same time as in that month she was writing that 'Coutts Lindsay has done all that an artist's eye can do to make it beautiful, and riches have made it comfortable'.[24]

If Coutts had been spending freely, reinforcement was close at hand. Blanche FitzRoy was now launched into society; she had been presented at a Drawing Room and Hannah had given a ball and a concert for her. A visit in November to Mentmore, the Buckinghamshire home of her uncle Baron Mayer Amschel de Rothschild, was a momentous affair ('All Mentmore is in commotion at the expected arrival of the FitzRoys') and Blanche's Aunt Charlotte, wife of Baron Lionel de Rothschild, Hannah's eldest brother, the owner of Gunnersbury Park, was the dispenser of Rothschild family information and the originator of all the observations made on her niece in the following account. She suspected that the FitzRoys would be very far from pleased when 'they see only Reverends and irreverends – I mean Caucasian beaux' – Aunt Charlotte's name for all Jews. She reported that not one word in admiration of Mentmore had been uttered, but that the Holfords were also guests and Robert Holford was expected to be surprised at the beauty of the building and its contents. This was most probably May's first introduction to Blanchy from which much would follow.

Of the cousins whom Blanche met there, Alice (the daughter of the young Rothschild bride whom Anne had met at Brondesbury in 1826) had found favour while Clementine, daughter of Aunt Charlotte's brother, was neither spoken of, nor spoken to. Blanche herself was looking brilliantly handsome but her mother had started on what would prove a fatal illness. According to her sister-in-law, Aunt Charlotte, she had an enormous swelling on her back like a camel's hump and quite hot too, her face white, shrunk and furrowed, shivery and trembling, expressive of intensive pain, but she would talk of nothing but parties and how Lord Loughborough hovered about her child, though not eligible as a husband. 'As she mentions no one else I suppose he is the only adorer.' Nevertheless Hannah, whose thoughts were constantly running upon marriage, was unremitting in her chaperoning; no doubt she was suffering martyrdom but she would have suffered as much at home if she had thought 'her Blanchy missed assemblies and balls and opportunities of making useful conquests'.

By now, April 1864, Blanche was pronounced infinitely less good-looking than during the past winter season, although at a Rothschild dinner party, wearing a muslin dress, lilies-of-the-valley in her hair and cherry-coloured ribbons, 'poor Blanche' had devoted herself to Lord Sefton before and during dinner. A few days later Hannah had spoken to her brother Lionel and his wife, Charlotte, of her child's adorers ('fortune-hunters I am afraid'). Passing in review all the young beaux of the present day she had said that not one could be considered worthy of Blanche: 'Lord Sefton and Lord Coventry she will not hear of, though I am not at all aware that they intend proposing.' However, the theme had developed on a grander scale when Blanche was taken to a ball by Virginia Somers (perhaps egged on to do so by May), and though cross to her relations whom she found there, 'flirted incessantly with unswerving devotion, and intense delight; the object of her favours was the heir to Blenheim Palace – the young lady would have no objection to becoming Marchioness of Blandford – and I think the Duchess of Marlborough would not object to the alliance.'[25]

For all her flirting with ducal heirs Blanche's future had been resolved already. On 9 May, to Aunt Charlotte's delight, her husband was summoned to his sister Hannah Mayer's bedside to consult with him, 'as a matter of form of course'. She wished to know whether he considered Sir Coutts Lindsay, Bt an eligible husband for her daughter.

20

Aunt Charlotte Reporting

The only obtainable account of Blanche's engagement is
from letters of her Aunt Charlotte de Rothschild to her
nineteen-year-old son Leopold, at Cambridge University,
and therefore quotations from these supply what information there is, offset and acidulated with a splash of lemon.[26]
That she was sorry for Hannah, one of her own race, and in
an invalid state, there is no doubt. Also pity, engendered
especially by Blanche's unfeeling behaviour towards her
mother after marriage; but she was inclined to deride
Hannah's pretensions for her daughter. There would be no
mercenary angling for her own daughter, Evelina, in the
following year; in fact it was most probably already an
inter-family concurrence that she would marry a cousin,
Ferdinand de Rothschild (the begetter of Waddesdon
Manor). But Evelina was not yet married and Blanchy, the
younger by five years, had stolen a march and had captured
the most fascinating of unmarried men who had eluded the
beauty and dignity of greater names. However, Charlotte
was not wanting in shrewdness and readily understood that
the financial provision which Blanche would bring with her
weighted the scales very much in her favour. Perhaps, too,
there was an element of real attachment on Coutts's part,
quickened by her patent and passionate love for him and by
the fact that she had not yet understood his all too public
admiration for Virginia Somers nor become aware of the
existence of his two unlawfully begotten children. That he
also had a mistress with whom he was known to be in love
was dismissed by Hannah and probably not repeated to the
prospective bride.

Blanche's first meeting with Coutts was presumably either at Little Holland House, conducted there by Virginia, or, more likely, at Dorchester House where Coutts was working and to which May Holford would have chaperoned her, both women acting in collusion to ensure Coutts's march to the altar. He was forty and a man of experience, Blanche twenty years younger and only latterly out in the world and freed from adolescent restraints. Seeing Coutts working at his designs for Dorchester House, engaged in work she could understand and probably flatteringly admire – this was indeed heady stuff. She was captivated by his way of life and bowled over by his charm of speech and manner towards her. She fell headlong in love.

Hannah had known nothing of what was hatching: meetings had been conducted in secret, lending further excitement to Blanche's new feeling of romantic independence. Her mother had not had the absorbing interest of watching the courtship which now progressed as recounted by Aunt Charlotte to her son. (In the first letter she is repeating what was told her by Hannah.)

9 May 1864. The Baronet has paid devoted attention to the young lady at his sister Mrs Holford's house. He has fallen desperately in love with your cousin, and she returns his affection. There is not one syllable to be said against him, but thousands of words would not exhaust the praise he merits. He is excellent and admirable in every relation of life, the most dutiful of sons, the most tenderly affectionate of brothers, the kindest of friends – and the most accomplished of men, good and clever, full of talent and highly cultivated, in short perfection – but not quite young; he is in his fortieth year, with a fine estate, ten thousand a year, and charming relatives. Of course he is passionately attached to Blanche, but his lovely sister, Mrs Holford, and his charming cousin Lady Somers, have sedulously fanned the flame. He proposed yesterday at 6, and is to call tomorrow at ½ past 12 for Blanche's reply. The answer will be in the affirmative.

10 May. Hannah Mayer completely overcome with her conflicting feelings; she had been crying and sobbing, almost shrieking. The marriage itself, *ceci entre nous*, does not satisfy her completely, for the bridgroom elect is forty and has grey locks, and perhaps her ambition would have soared higher and selected a nobleman with a grand title for her daughter. Exhausted with pain while the great event of her daughter's life, her courtship and betrothal, are filling Blanche's heart with rapturous happiness. She gave a gracious reception to Sir Coutts Lindsay this-morning, spoke a few words to Mrs Holford and received a bright cheering visit from Lady Somers – but she could not make up her mind to see Lady Lindsay and Mrs Lindsay and the new family. Evy [Evelina] says that she feels jealous of her daughter's affection for all the strangers and that being very ill she becomes unhappy and hysterical. Lord and Lady Somers and the Holfords are perfectly enchanted, whether the rest of the world will sympathize, remains to be seen.

11 May. Everybody says Sir Coutts is an angel, perfectly charming, wonderfully good, marvellously clever, but an angel with white hair, twenty years older than his bride elect. She is much in love and in a sort of paradise – she listens to all the pretty speeches which fall from the lips of his relatives. Mrs Holford keeps repeating that she will never require a drawing master nor he a model.

12 May. We returned Mrs Holford's visit, and Mrs Lindsay's cards, and I spent hours by Aunt H.M.'s bedside. She does not know what she wants exactly – what she regrets, what she would have preferred – but to Blanche she scarcely speaks, though she thinks of nothing but the trousseau, and the price it is to cost. The marriage is to be soon, and the young people are to go to Scotland for the autumn and to Rome for the winter.

13 May. Sir Coutts Lindsay called this-afternoon to see Papa, and made himself very agreeable. Sir Coutts has very handsome features and a decidedly agreeable expression, but he is very peculiar looking, his hair being perfectly grey. He wants Papa to ask when the wedding may take place; your father means to depute Evy to put the question, no easy one, to Aunt H.M., who will not hear of the sacred ceremony by special licence and means Blanche to be married in church.

17 May. Aunt H.M. seemed much relieved at having gone through much trying and fatiguing business with the lawyer. Marriage contracts, settlements and Wills are matters fraught with anxiety even when under the most auspicious circumstances. She was pleased with Sir Coutts Lindsay, who far from objecting to anything, declared that all Mrs FitRoy's arrangements were perfect and that he never thought and could never think of Blanche's money; that without one penny she would be equally dear and precious to him. 'I was angry with Blanche for having settled everything without me, who have lived only for her', said Aunt H.M., 'but I cannot be angry with her any more as he is the most fascinating person I ever met.' She will, I think, consent to have the ceremony solemnized in the drawing-room. She could not go to church, and it would kill her to see Blanche leave the house without her. Sir Coutts Lindsay, though engaged upwards of ten days, has not been able to find in all this enormous London one tiny ring to bestow upon his bride. He says that he has ordered something for her. It seems that the world does not malign the Lindsays.

18 May. Sir Coutts Lindsay has given a very handsome ring to Blanche – the setting is commonplace but the stones are fine and Aunt H.M. admires them.

21 May. She [H.M.] thinks that Sir Coutts is a wonder of generosity and every day, poor woman, she tells me of the beauty of the ruby ring. He has ordered a pony phaeton, and that is thought quite wonderful.

23 May. Today we have been inspecting the novelties prepared for the season by the great jewellers of this town but we have not decided upon any wedding presents. Whatever we select for Blanche is sure to be thought ugly and that certainly is somewhat disheartening.

25 May. I am afraid that Blanche will not receive many presents: she has so few friends, except the English Rothschilds, a few of the continental R[othschild]s, I really do not know who is to give her anything. The Lindsays have not the reputation of being generous, but 'love works wonders', and Sir Coutts may shower pearls and diamonds upon her; at present he has given her two rings. Aunt H.M. is becoming more and more reconciled to the marriage – and is never weary of enumerating the advantages of the bridegroom's position to which she will lend the additional charms of youth and beauty, and many feminine talents and attractions. Tonight Mrs Holford opens her splendid house; the reception is said to take place in honour of Blanche, who is not allowed to attend it and who wanted Evy to intercede in her favour with Aunt H.M. The bridesmaids' lockets are ordered and Evy is to be one of the wearers.

26 *May.* We saw Blanche today in a private hansom with Sir Coutts Lindsay. She looked radiantly happy, and her colouring both delicate and brilliant; he is certainly fascinating with beautiful features and his appearance is original and picturesque. Aunt H.M. ought to be satisfied.

1 June. Blanche rushed down into the drawing-room shortly after our arrival to welcome the sister-in-law of Sir Coutts Lindsay, Mrs Loyd-Lindsay. I caught a glimpse of the lady, who looks pleasing and clever and distinguished and has the reputation of being quite charming. I rather fancy Aunt H.M. is vexed that no one takes any notice of Blanche and her engagements – but she has had few opportunities, poor girl, of making acquaintances and fewer still of making friends. As for presents, were I a sporting character, I would willingly bet that she will not recive as many as ten from non-Rothschilds and non-Lindsays. By the bye, the bridegroom elect has given nothing except two rings – and he has ordered a pony-chaise but that is a present for himself as well as for his bride.

4 June. We saw old Mrs Lindsay, who was with Blanche in the drawing-room, but she is young Mrs Lindsay without false teeth and with brown hair. Blanche's new Mamma was very courteous, but rather tiresome. The young lady showed us a present from her silver-haired adorer, an Indian necklace, but without pearls or precious stones. I like it much, but Aunt H.M. does not consider it worthy of her daughter and of the occasion. I have found a pretty locket and chain for the fair bride elect, but I think I shall be obliged to select a souvenir of each of you three, and really it is a matter of some difficulty. Evy has just come back from a family dinner at 107[27] [Piccadilly] where old Mrs Lindsay was stately and smiling; Uncle Mayer uncertain, Lord Somers and Sir Coutts talkative, the Countess Virginia out of sorts, and Blanche though radiant-looking, by no means communicative. She asked for a repetition under this roof, and I suppose we must grant her request.

6 June. Towards evening when we were both at home, Sir Coutts Lindsay called and talked of nothing but art and pictures; he is decidedly agreeable though somewhat *einseitig.* * Evy may choose a beautiful locket to be given in Aunt Charlotte's name – Natty wishes to be generous –therefore Blanche will have plenty of Rothschild presents to make up for the lack of others.[28]

8 June. Paying a visit to poor H.M. who is much tormented as – but this is a secret – those who ought to act in a noble, disinterested, chivalrous spirit, show themselves very mean.

9 June. Your father accompanied by Evelina went to Garrard's this-morning to select presents for Blanche. He and Uncle Nat are to give plate. He may also buy a handsome ornament to be presented in Aunt Charlotte's name, and Uncle James has sent £150 to Alfy to invest in any way he pleases for Miss FitzRoy. Every thing has become fearfully expensive and nothing seems to produce any effect – but we must do our best.

Might the reason for so rushed a marriage lie in the fear that Coutts's affection might waver and cool; or else that Hannah's probable imminent death would throw Blanche into months of mourning, enabling Coutts to go off with the Somerses on another yachting excursion? Two months' preparation for money transactions to be effected and trousseau ordered was little enough time at that period. Also, during her engagement certain facts relative to Coutts's past and present had been brought to light and objections made. The stronger the criticisms from her relations, the stronger Blanche's resolve, and in this she was only echoing her mother's determination of twenty-five years ago.

We know little of the reactions of the large family of Lindsays. The Holfords of course were strongly in favour, having connived at it. Harriet Loyd-Lindsay had asked

*One-sided.

Anne during the engagement 'what the "family" do about calling or leaving cards on the Rothschilds. Of course I should like to do what is considered right and what Coutts wishes.' At first the engagement had been something of a shock to Anne: not what she had dreamed of for the young man who once seemed to have greatness within his grasp. But in a short time she had been won by Blanche's obvious 'true loving heart. I cant think now, why we made ourselves so needlessly unhappy,' she told Minnie, who replied that by all accounts Blanche must be attractive and lovable.

21

Blanche Lindsay

Unfortunately, since Leopold was now at home for the vacation, there is no first-hand account of the wedding day. The marriage was held on 30 June 1864 in the drawing-room of Upper Grosvenor Street, Blanche arrayed in white and the Revd Evan Nepean, Canon of Westminster, officiating. Hannah was too ill to leave her bed, but Anne Lindsay, Angela Burdett-Coutts, Lord Somers, Viscount Bury (a cousin of Coutts), and the seventeen-year-old James Ludovic Lindsay, eldest son of Minnie and Lindsay, were witnesses; Lord Southampton, Blanche's uncle, was the only representative on her side.

For the first three weeks the newly-wed couple remained at Brighton and elsewhere, going only to Scotland at the end of July by which time Balcarres would have been made ready for them. Leopold was absent from home soon after the wedding so that his mother's correspondence was speedily resumed. But by now Aunt Charlotte's temperate liking for her niece receded into something akin to hostility, partly owing to Blanche's lack of consideration for her mother and partly, perhaps, to something patronizing in the new bride. That she was very pleased with her married name, which in society set her above her mother-in-law, was all too evident.

After marriage Blanche isolated herself almost entirely from the Rothschilds, always excepting her friendship for her cousin Constance whom she saw not infrequently in London in Grosvenor Place, and at Aston Clinton. It was all a rejection of her Jewish background, even though the Rothschilds were the only people who had been behind her, albeit a shade disapprovingly, from the time of her launch into society.

Just a week after the wedding Coutts came to London ostensibly for the wedding of a friend. Blanche had stayed behind, perhaps not wishing to call on her mother. The Rothschilds were also at the wedding party and Aunt Charlotte continues the narrative.

7 July. I told a deliberate falsehood but it was a benevolent untruth. 'Is it true', said H.M. suddenly, 'that Sir Coutts absented himself and was not present at the breakfast?' 'I was not in the dining-room and did not see who surrounded the table.' A confirmation of the suspected truth would have made your aunt perfectly frantic.

8 July. Evy, who has as many eyes as the busy bee, saw Sir Coutts Lindsay's brougham yesterday and himself in it near Princes Terrace,[29] the brougham remained stationed in those regions the whole afternoon – but Blanche did not come to town; I always thought her utterly heartless and though sorry to find my opinion confirmed – I am glad to find I am not harsh and unjust in my surmise. Lady Somers told Evy the Rothschilds had been heard to speak against the bridegroom and that it had been reported to Mr and Mrs Holford. Your sister answered the evil-speaking as an impossibility for we do not even know Sir Coutts Lindsay not having seen him or spoken to him more than two or three times.

11 July. Lady Lindsay, née FitzRoy has not yet been to see her suffering mother but speaks of coming at the end of the week. We have asked her to dine here on Saturday, and thus the chapter of our civilities to the bride and bridegroom will end.

12 July. Evy, in answer to a few lines from Lady Lindsay, asked the heartless bride to come and see her mother. She has the impudence to speak of a journey of three hours duration – but is nevertheless coming tomorrow. Strange to say, Aunt H.M. tells everyone that she now misses her long-lost husband infinitely more than her absent daughter – who during two or three months which preceeded her marriage became quite estranged from her.

13 July. Evy again met Sir Coutts Lindsay near Prince's Terrace.

14 July. We called as usual on Mrs FitzRoy – not much cheered by the arrival of Lady Lindsay who does not seem to devote much time to the invalid. In the course of another week she will again have left London. What a heartless serpent that unfortunate Mrs F[itzRoy] has reared in her bosom.

16 July. Lady Lindsay is quite as affected and namby pamby as before her marriage; with so much talent and so many rare gifts and accomplishments a little nature would be most desirable to produce a really charming ensemble. Lady Lindsay was an icicle yesterday.

19 July. Sir Coutts and Lady Lindsay took lunch here to-day. He made himself agreeable, and, on leaving shook hands most energetically. She really looked handsome – almost beautiful in repose; when she smiles or laughs, she does not give one the idea of wisdom, or wit or genuine mirth. As she is wonderfully clever she might have spoken, but she did not condescend to open her lips.

22 July. Blanche paid her farewell visit, she leaves tomorrow for Scotland with the intention of coming back in six weeks to see her mother. Only think, Evy actually had the courage to tell Lady Somers that if Aunt H.M. had taken a dislike to her, it is because she suspects Sir Coutts to have been her admirer. This the lady emphatically denied, declaring that she loves 'Eastnor' and has never been capable of any flirtation in the whole course of her life – but she added energetically: 'Sir Coutts is my dearest friend – were he my brother I could not feel more sincerely attached to him, but had he been the object of a warmer feeling, I should not have married him to Blanche!'

30 July. Lady Lindsay's letter to her mother is admirably written, full of tenderness, devotion, delicate compliments, graceful and ending with a prayer for the invalid's speedy and complete recovery. What a horrible humbug and heartless hypocrite Blanche Lady Lindsay is.

16 August. Blanche seems enchanted with her possessions, beginning let us hope, with her husband, and ending with her romantic words.

Blanche's first letter from Balcarres was a long one, beginning with loving thoughts for her mother, fretting about her health, repeating her willingness to come immediately to London if needed. 'I feel I have made a happy choice,' she continued, 'and one which I do not think I shall ever have cause to regret, at least so far as human eyes can see.' She was immensely attracted to Balcarres and she and Coutts planned various alterations. Among others in the house, a large, high-ceilinged room above the dining-room, originally meant for billiards, was promptly redesigned as Coutts's studio. Unexpectedly, while looking through some of his many canvases, Blanche came upon a sketch head in oils of a young woman – undoubtedly her own mother. To her huge surprise Coutts had bought it after Scheffer's death from his studio, not knowing the identity of the sitter. It had been begun when Hannah Mayer Rothschild had been enjoying her first ball in Paris in 1834 and had hastily been sent packing when Prince Edmond de Clary had declared his love.

In the Oak Room the sixteenth-century ceiling had been newly coloured blue with raised gilt mouldings; below it, oak panels would before long be fitted into the surrounding walls incorporating figures representing the Labours of Hercules.

The magical terraced garden designed by Coutts was to be one of the glories of Balcarres. He took as a guide the eighteenth-century *Les Jardins du Roi de Pologne* – and part of his wife's marriage portion to defray the cost. Magnificent, with a double stairway leading to a garden of sharply clipped pyramids of box and a formal parterre of partitions of box enclosing brilliantly coloured flowers, the whole backed by a long and dense wall of yew hedging higher than a man. Beds of flowers within finely cut hedges of yew and box, a further single staircase, arcades and alleyways, all strictly formal and of great beauty, brought this evergreen garden to perfection.

Blanche, writing to her mother, criticized the dairy as not 'picturesque', though explaining that it was 'not a poetical dairy', nevertheless she lapped a little cream. The laundry, well equipped with excellent presses, was satisfactory, also the drying grounds. After driving to Elie they had walked over rocks to a sheltered cove where to Blanche's own astonishment she had actually taken off her shoes and stockings, hitched up her crinoline dress and petticoats 'in a most rustic way', and had danced about on the edge of the tiny waves as they gently rippled the sand. It is the voice of a happy young woman.

In the photographs taken in the garden at Balcarres that autumn, Blanche stands beside her jaded-looking husband, one hand holding her fur-trimmed jacket against the Scottish breezes, the other a small feathered bonnet. There is a hint of a little smile, giving a sweetness to her face and an expression to the eyes that bears out a Lindsay cousin's description of her, when she was first married, as a clever, amusing, very high-spirited, giggling girl – a tom-boy girl, who spoke (certainly in later years) in an almost inaudible falsetto which would suddenly burst into a shattering laugh as of a train shooting, whistling, out of a tunnel – peal upon peal emitted by a very strong sense of humour. In Coutts, seated on a stone balustrade beneath a leafless tree and looking at Blanche as she turns away her head, it is possible to catch something of affection as he leans towards her. Her youth and adoration must have touched this still fascinating middle-aged roué – for so he appears in Julia Cameron's photograph of a year later. The desire to improve the house, to lay out the gardens and to have the financial means to do so would have been a happy prospect. Besides which, this month of September was the first month of Blanche's pregnancy. She would give Balcarres an heir, he would cherish his wife, and there would be no need to relinquish the beguiling Virginia Somers. The same Lindsay cousin had been led to believe that 'Countess Somers, the beautiful

"Virginia", engineered the engagement as Coutts was for ever at her beck and call.' She judged this marriage would draw a cloak of respectability over her close intimacy with the handsome Coutts.

Blanche had decided to build a little school for girls to learn needlework at which she herself was particularly skilled. Soon she would start a library for the villagers in a wing of the castle, with the local grocer in command. The most eager of the readers were the colliers of the neighbourhood.

There were outside diversions to write about. A visit to neighbours in the dashing dark blue pony chaise picked out in red, with rosettes on the horses' heads to match, which had been Blanche's wedding present. There she had met Harriet Hosmer, the American sculptress who had her own studio in Rome. A masculine woman, 'thinking no end of her own forehead', from which she would brush her dark, very short hair 'à la Rosa Bonheur'. But Blanche was amused by her and found her pleasant. Dining with other neighbours – and this was the first time she had ever gone out to dinner in the country – she had thought of wearing her pale blue silk dress with her pearls, and white rice-paper convolvulus in her hair, but since they were obliged to hire a fly, the only one thereabouts – having nothing but the open pony carriage – she had decided on what she considered was an appropriate and matronly costume, low at the neck, with short sleeves and a long train. Her small well-shaped head was wreathed with crimson carnations. She felt herself of some consequence when as a bride she was taken in with due ceremony by her host who carved the turbot and mutton himself, according to country custom, and to her surprise.

On 11 August: 'Mrs Lindsay just arrived here.' Otherwise Blanche would send presents of fruit and flowers to her mother from Scotland, only, that as Aunt Charlotte observed, 'the poor invalid cannot eat fruit any longer and finds the perfume of roses at times over-powering.'

At the end of the month Coutts and she were at Dunecht with Minnie and Lord Lindsay. Blanche thought him 'a most amiable man', a scholar and very learned, but he was always hidden behind a folio and was short-sighted to an uncommon degree. What chiefly impressed her was the extraordinary effect made by turnips planted nearly up to the house and on every side so as to make the grass grow better another year. To see garden, trees, and shrubs in the midst of a field of turnips was an amazement to someone who would have been more at home in her uncles' estates of Aston Clinton, Gunnersbury, or Mentmore.

22

Death of Mrs FitzRoy

The end of September saw the Lindsays' return to London from Balcarres and Aunt Charlotte continued her correspondence with Leopold.

3 October 1864. I said [to Hannah Mayer] I had heard much of Blanche's looks of rosy health and beauty and happiness but she did not respond to my compliment with any degree of enthusiasm. It was *three* when I left and the unnatural daughter had not yet called. [Except for her doctor, H.M. had seen no one for seven weeks.] Lady Lindsay did not make an appearance yesterday.

12 October. I drove to Bond Street and whom should I see but Blanche Lady Lindsay with that peculiar expression of countenance which seems to set at nought all the laws of physiognomy and phrenology. How can a person so highly and so brilliantly gifted, and whose talents have been so admirably and so successfully developed, look so intensely silly and foolish. Sir Coutts and Lady Lindsay are going to Italy – at least I see an announcement to that effect in the papers, and Lord and Lady Somers who are, I believe in London, will probably follow. Lady Lindsay [whom Evy saw] and thinks beamingly handsome, and so beautifully dressed 'with rings on her fingers' as in the nursery ballad – adoring her Coutts. All the friends are in London before they start for Italy probably, Lord and Lady Warwick, Lord and Lady Lindsay, Mr and Mrs Holford, the enchanting Countess Virginia and her little gnome of a husband.

19 October [from Brighton]. The novelties yesterday were four visitors, viz. Sir Coutts and Lady Lindsay, Prince Gortschakoff and Mr Sabouroff of the Russian Embassy. Blanche was a perfect picture, though more brilliant than if her husband had painted it – for his style is mediaeval, and his forte lies in beauty of expression, not of colouring. One, nay two feelings did she express – enthusiastic love for her husband, and radiant happiness. I really never saw her look so bright, so dazzling. [Your cousin's toilette] was the perfection of an English great lady's costume – soft Scottish materials falling in graceful folds. Tomorrow Sir Coutts and Lady Lindsay return to London for a week or ten days, and then they go to Italy. Lord and Lady Somers are also to spend the winter in the land of my childhood and youth. Lord S. is already in Milan, but her ladyship tarries here ostensibly to select a governess, the fourth within three months – in reality, I suspect not to be too far away from those whose happiness is her work. The loving couple are to be our guests at dinner this evening, and we have asked the two Russian secretaries to join them – not a very charming addition, but there are no social resources at Brighton. Blanche would not have appreciated Judea. You can have no idea of how handsome Sir Coutts Lindsay has become, his complexion is so much clearer and fairer and he is now so scrupulously clean.

26 October. Lady Lindsay has an obstinate cold and writes long letters to her mama from Grosvenor Square instead of driving to Upper Grosvenor Street.

30 October. We were perhaps a little too severe upon Blanche who has the hooping cough *badly*. She called yesterday in Upper Grosvenor Street and had a paroxysm which lasted a quarter of an hour.

3 November. [Blanche, with whooping cough, was with her mother.] Sir Coutts was downstairs, pacing up and down the pavement. He said: 'She will not see me. I am not a favourite.' And then Blanche said: 'The doctors wish to send me to Italy; they think I shall never get rid of my cough, unless I seek a warmer climate.' Lady Somers leaves on Tuesday, therefore I suppose that Sir Coutts is becoming impatient. What a strange wicked heartless world this is.

5 November. Blanche much worn by spasmodic cough and immensely happy at being Lady Lindsay, and far too much so, to feel deep anxiety for her suffering and perhaps dying mother. Sir Coutts has resumed his artist-life. At an early hour he hurries off to his studio and his easel, not however without Blanche, who has her pencils and palette, her piano and music, and the whole day to spend in delightful pursuits. Blanche makes one great mistake; she

copies Lady Somers's style of headdress and her new dresses are also a very servile – they cannot be a faithful – imitation of that beautiful Siren's costume. Black silk, slashed with black velvet, copied from some Venetian print or picture of a Doge's wife painted by Titian,[30] does not suit your cousin – and Sir Coutts cannot do otherwise than establish involuntary and dangerous comparisons.

16 November. Blanche arrives at 5 o'clock in the evening, stays 5 minutes and then departs. Do not mention this heartless behaviour as it is a perfect disgrace to our family, and must shock the domestics from whom constant fidelity is expected.

17 November. H.M. was visible only to that horrible Blanche, who upon the plea that the invalid is too weak to bear even her adored presence beyond 5 or 6 minutes in the course of the day, never puts her foot into the house before 5 o'clock in the evening, viz not before the shades of evening put an end to her drawing in Sir Coutts Lindsay's studio; then she arrives, novel in hand, while her unfortunate mother carries on the unequal battle with disease and death.

21 November. Blanche is in bed but Sir Coutts called last evening and was admitted to the bedside of the sufferer.

23 November. Poor Aunt H.M. looks dying; it is heart-rending to see the sufferer – no one can be unmoved and unconcerned, except Blanche. We thought it our duty, Aunt Anthony and I, to pay Blanche a visit, because she was reported to be ill in bed. We found her in the drawing-room on the sofa – ordered to take care of herself for family reasons, but – I will not write smiling – the word it too good for the heartless staring creature, giggling and grinning and simpering, while she asked after her dying mother as if the poor sufferer had had a mere cold. She told us her visits to H.M. have been too much for her strength, and I own I was amazed at the impudence of the assertion!

25 November. H.M. reduced to a skeleton. Motionless, and can neither speak nor bear conversation above a whisper and unable to read her daughter's letters. Blanche remains interesting, on a sofa and Sir Coutts now calls once in twenty-four hours – probably to tell the suffering woman of her child's bright hopes.

27 *November.* H.M. implored her sister to go to Grosvenor Square and beg Blanche not on any account to endanger her precious hopes by coming to see her. Aunt Lou[ise] felt far too indignant at the conduct of the unnatural daughter to pay her a friendly visit, but she drove to the house, and asked Sir Coutts to come out and receive the message. She thought him old and ugly, but though very grey, he is undoubtedly handsome, if fine features, an intellectual appearance and a gentleman-like bearing constitute good looks.

2 *December.* Hannah Mayer is sinking. 'Send quickly for Lady Lindsay.' H.M. kissed and blessed her child repeatedly and asked when the expected baby would be born, begged the darling, God bless it, might receive a pretty name.

Hannah's death (and she had a terror of being buried alive) released Blanche from her mother's family though scarcely from her aunt's epistolary judgements.

3 *December.* All property [including jewels, furs, plate left] to Blanche and she has named Sir Coutts and the lawyer her executors. The Will was drawn up the week before last, immediately after your poor Aunt had seen Sir Coutts. I am glad no Rothschild has been consulted or mentioned – thus there can be no pretext for any disagreement.

4 *December.* The funeral to be on the 9th.

6 *December.* I drove to Grosvenor Square. Blanche was stretched out on a most comfortable sofa, giving directions to one of poor Aunt H.M.'s faithful servants. When we were left alone, she renewed her thanks for my attention to her mother, and then spoke of her own health, which she said would oblige her to go out of town; not until after the last mournful ceremony, was my reply. 'Oh! yes – I cannot be of any use – Coutts wishes me to go, the Doctor insists upon it – and I am not going to any scene of gaiety – only to Lockinge, to stay with my sister-in-law, Mrs Loyd-Lindsay, who has just lost her own mother; we shall be a great comfort and consolation to each other.' I do not believe that Blanche is strong; she looked nervous and was twitching her head, much as usual – but consolation she does not require. Her drawings and paintings, pencils and brushes were lying about her,

and evidently the charming pursuits of an artist, and even a musician had not been interrupted during the last weeks when her poor mother's final struggle may be said to have commenced. The Duchess of Grafton, Lady Louisa Charteris, Lady Warwick, and, 'last though not least' Mrs Holford, are all in town – consequently Blanche's pretext for going out of town, proves worthless; she said that Coutts would be busy, and could not bear the idea of leaving her alone; she would not have been solitary, any more than she has been hitherto, for her friends have crowded round her – and would gladly have dispelled the gloom of her loneliness.

10 *December*. Alfred ['Alfy' de Rothschild] said that the funeral ceremony was short and not imposing. He was in a carriage with the Duke of Grafton, Lord Charles FitzRoy and Lord Southampton who had known and seen the deceased so little, that they never alluded to her but talked of rail-roads, horses etc. Aunt H.M. did not seem to remember she had seven thousand at her bankers. These savings she need not have given Sir Coutts.

22 *December*. Today there are two letters from Lady Lindsay, one to Papa asking for a carriage from Boulogne to Paris. The lady and her husband leave this-evening for the continent.

Anne Lindsay was in Florence (as were the Somerses) when Lady Duff Gordon wrote that Coutts and Blanche were to start on the 22nd for Florence. 'He looks much worn. Hope Blanche will stand the journey well. Should not expect her to be a good traveller but she will have every comfort and kindness money can produce.'

This was Blanche's first introduction to Italy and it was here that she began to copy Old Masters. They went first to Genoa, buying fine old silks and chair covers; Trento to Riva and Saló in a horse shay, and finally to Florence. Before leaving England, Blanche had quietly arranged (no doubt with Coutts's help) to sell the portraits of her Rothschild grandparents, but to her exasperation her manoeuvre had been discovered by none other than Aunt Charlotte.

4 *February*. The portraits of your grandparents arrived yesterday from Upper Grosvenor Street. They cost ten pounds. How could

Lady Lindsay part with them. A lady, great and rich and, one would think, not yet hardened by the world – to sell her grandmother and her grandfather; it is not to be believed.

10 February. Uncle Anthony has received a letter from Blanche Lindsay, who states – rather late in the day, but better late than never – that she does not wish to sell her grandfather and her grandmother; I suppose she thought she might dispose of them in a clandestine manner and never expected that we should hear of the Sale and become the purchasers.

Four months in Italy in 1865 renewed Blanche's strength and assured her an easy pregnancy. For Coutts it was all enchantment. In Florence his mother, Minnie and Lindsay were there to welcome them. Rome followed and in March they were in Naples with the Somerses as constant companions. Aunt Charlotte heard from others that Blanche was admired, was perfectly charming and courteous beyond description. 'But', her aunt observed, 'she is scarcely in mourning.'

23

Three Births

Their return to London had been effected a week before the birth of the baby, Euphemia (Effie), on 15 May. Charlotte de Rothschild's pen, meanwhile, had not lain idle.

8 May 1865. Sir Coutts Lindsay was in London to make domestic arrangements. He has not one single brown hair left, and Blanche who expects her infant on the 10th will be here next Tuesday or Thursday, so says Mrs Holford. The Lindsays have taken Lord Huntly's shooting box in the Highlands but not for themselves alone. Lord and Lady Somers are to accompany them on the 12th of August.

13 May. The other early visitor was Blanche Lady Lindsay, all smiles, all radiance of colouring, less affected than before her marriage, evidently immensely happy and certainly pretty, graceful and distinguished looking especially in repose; when she speaks her teeth are large and look yellow and the expression of her countenance is not clever. She was not communicative and talked neither of her travels, nor of her stay abroad.

16 May. Blanche had not a single article of clothing in the house for the reception of her baby – nor was there a nurse. Will the newborn be called Virginia?

24 May. Lady Somers is afraid of the brigands of Ischia and Naples and is haring back to England. I had a presentiment that she could not stay away many months from her beloved Coutts.

In London Coutts had had his studio in the Grosvenor Square house where they were living on their return

from their Scottish summer. It was kept bare and un-
furnished to accommodate large canvases and designs for
Dorchester House, for Coutts had now launched into a
studio in Cromwell Place, South Kensington. This was a
1859 development; the road was a private one running
south from Cromwell Road to Onslow Crescent (now the
site of Melton Court) and could be shut off. Two stuccoed
houses on the east side at the northern end were occupied as
studios, Lord Somers having had a studio there as early as
1861; and facing, at No. 7, Millais and his wife had been the
first occupants since the same year.

The Coutts Lindsays had been considering a house of
their own, away from Mayfair and the Lindsay families.
No. 11 Grosvenor Square was nominally Anne's and
naturally enough Blanche wished for an establishment of
her own, although Anne was fond of her – 'a dear loving
little thing', she was calling her in 1865. That year the
architect and developer, C. J. Freake, sold one of the two
houses for £4,700 which, when united with its neighbour,
would meet the requirements of a town house. It was an
attractive proposition, lying in a part of London more
associated with the fine arts. The South Kensington
Museum was building; Leighton, the friend from Roman
days, was moving into his recently designed house in
Holland Park Road; Watts was installed in Little Holland
House, Val Prinsep was not far away; but to Coutts, at any
rate, the particular draw must have been that close by, in
Princes Gate at the top of Exhibition Road, the Somerses
had established themselves at No. 33.

When acquiring the two houses, No. 5, consisting of a
basement and one square storey over, was left as it was,[31]
while No. 4 was heightened, adding a floor and an attic and
dormer windows behind the parapet. The stabling was at
the back. The interiors won enthusiastic approval; Virginia,
while saying that Blanche was the dullest of womankind,
nevertheless agreed that her house was the loveliest one

could see, that the drawing-room was full of her turquoise-blue Sèvres which she told everyone had belonged to her mother.

Meanwhile Anne, writing an affectionate letter to Blanche from La Spezia, asked about Effie's vaccination, 'a bright, merry and intelligent child', and hoped she would resemble Blanche's family in looks, for at Mentone on her way south she had seen Lady Marian Alford who lived chiefly abroad and was still there later in the year when Carlyle arrived to be Louisa Ashburton's guest at the Villa Madonna. She had spoken affectionately of Blanche's father, Henry FitzRoy, who had been one of her dear friends and had said that Hannah had been 'quite lovely, like a Rafaele madonna. Adieu, dearest Blanche. Give my love to your and my dear Coutts. Tell me a great deal about him when you write.'

Blanche was enjoying her London life enormously. She had been able to buy shares for Coutts in the Wigan Coal and Iron Company, a recent amalgamation of small pits including the larger Haigh pit, and this had pleased him, though he was said to have been looking bored at a dinner party, since he loved only the fine arts and human nature in the shape of the incomparable Virginia. At a Court ball in 1866, Blanche, wearing all her mother's emeralds and diamonds and beautifully dressed, was much admired as Lady Lindsay of Balcarres. In the late spring at the Private View of the Royal Academy Summer Exhibition where Coutts's portrait of May was on show, Blanche in a pink bonnet looked happy; she had been spending the whole day in the gallery, 'but her husband was far away. How could he leave his young wife,' Aunt Charlotte mused, 'barely twenty-one, quite alone in that crowd?' Later in the summer, unaccompanied by Coutts but with fine diamond stars in her bonnet, Blanche had driven down to an evening party at Chiswick House. 'The enchantress still lingers in London.' Virginia had had a persistent fever which had

Blanche Lindsay playing the violin, 1877

Amalfi

Landscape with figures

Painted plate after a design by Coutts Lindsay, 1862
The Grosvenor Gallery, west gallery

The Grosvenor Gallery, 1877

Coutts and Blanche Lindsay, Beaulieu, 1877

Blanche Lindsay, c. 1883

Coutts Lindsay outside the Grosvenor Gallery, 1883

given her a pallid appearance and Aunt Charlotte had found it impossible not to feel that even when bereft of freshness and brilliance she was a dangerous rival to the really gifted and distinguished Blanche with her simpering ways and silly laugh.

In airing her views on her niece, Aunt Charlotte was exercising her own particular brand of truthfulness which allowed little for human foibles. It was an alliance of recognition of what was best in Blanche, while heartily criticizing what she found objectionable. There was little of affection except perhaps what she owed to Hannah's memory. A further veiled disapproval was conveyed by particulars of Blanche's manner of dress: 'She wears neither cuffs, nor collars, nor crinoline, but mediaeval Italian sweeping skirts and innumerable chains, lockets, rings, bracelets, embroidered girdles and all the paraphernalia of Pre-Raphaelite pictures.' Her feeling for Virginia was more admiration than approbation, and, like many others, she was beguiled by the charm 'the enchantress' exerted – a commodity lacking in Blanche. 'Lady Somers walked into the room – an apparition of loveliness, having recovered her health and all its blessings, roses and vivacity, lilies and sparkling eyes and smiles and ringing laugh. How is it possible [she wondered] that Sir Coutts should love Blanche after having been enamoured of the enchanting Virginia?'

With Coutts she had never found an easy relationship and he had probably made no effort to help. When Alfred Wigan, the actor, returned from a stay at Balcarres, he was 'overloaded by the hospitable Baronet with Highland roses and peaches; so our cousin is less stingy and more amiable in Scotland than he was in London.' But Anne had been glad to have been at Balcarres that summer with her son and daughter-in-law. Harriet Loyd-Lindsay, who would always be a partisan of Blanche, delighted in the thought of Anne going to Eastnor which would be looking more beautiful than in the winter. 'Impressions of places have a good deal to do with the people who live there and Virginia would make any place sunny.'

From Gunnersbury Park in September 1866 Charlotte de Rothschild had written to her son Leopold regarding the weakness in the eyes from which Blanche was suffering. Gunnersbury was the large Italianate villa close to Kew and Acton bought by Nathan Mayer Rothschild in the 1830s, inherited by his eldest son, Baron Lionel, and passing in time to his own son Leopold.[32] Built in 1802, but with Rothschild's acquisition enlarged by Sydney Smirke to a three-storied house of stucco with wings and colonnaded loggia running between them, it overlooked fine parkland and fields. Stables had been built, also Gothick 'ruins' with which to conceal them. A Smirke orangery survives by the lake while an eighteenth-century temple by the round pond, possibly built as an ornamental dairy, is a reminder of the earlier life of the property when it had belonged to Princess Amelia, daughter of George III. While Jewish holy days which fell in the autumn were held at Gunnersbury, this little temple, modified and enlarged, acted as a synagogue. 'Without any exaggeration', Charlotte wrote on that September day, 'Gunnersbury looks like a paradise, trees, shrubs, flowers and green sward, smiling from daybreak till dusk in the unveiling, golden light of glowing sunshine.'

Her account of Blanche's eyes was more sombre. She could neither read, write, nor draw or paint – an enormous deprivation, given her talents in all these subjects; and unless she knew the piece by heart her violin playing was for the time being in abeyance. She could still travel, however, and November found her at Ford Castle, Louisa Waterford's Northumberland home ('though Sir Coutts was seen in town yesterday'). There she had been shown the murals in the little village school executed by Louisa.

Eveline de Rothschild had died in early December and as a first cousin of both Constance de Rothschild had paid a visit to Cromwell Place shortly after the funeral. But though

Blanche seemed to grieve, 'I do not think it was a real shock for her. She has not much feeling of that I am quite sure.' A couple of months later, Aunt Charlotte (the bereaved mother) was voicing her complaint of another visitor.

18 February 1867. Lady Somers came, very pale and agitated, full of kindness and sympathy and spent several hours here, partly with me, and partly with dear Papa, dwelling most lovingly on all our poor Eve's charming qualities and endearing ways. Though she, no doubt, was full of pity and sympathy for us, she forgot that she did not wear the garb of mourning, which she might have remembered as she was coming to our house of affliction. No one expected funeral crape, but she wore bright green and bright scarlet and white and fashionable cinnamon coloured silk slashed with satin − colours I have not seen for many weeks past.

Although Coutts had completed most of his work for Dorchester House there was the staircase still to finish. Nevertheless a great ball was held there in June, 'its dazzling brilliancy' unsurpassed; the house, full of magnificent pictures, was brilliantly lighted and 'sonorous with strains of enchanting music'. Coutts and his wife were at St Moritz in the Engadine with the Holfords in August, perhaps for Blanche to take chalybeate baths as a corrective to infertility − it was more than two years since her daughter had been born and there was the need of a (legitimate) son and heir. But Aunt Charlotte had her spies out.

12 August. French, German and English royalties have congregated at St Maurice. The beautiful Virginia has made her appearance at the steel springs, but Blanche and Sir Coutts, as I suspected, are not likely to arrive just yet.

14 August. The beautiful Virginia graciously invited Ferdy[33] and his brother to accompany her on an excursion in the mountains; it was her last free day, Sir Coutts was expected with the gifted and accomplished Blanche, who, most undeniably suffers from weak eyes.

The friendship seemingly so well cemented between Blanche and Virginia was wearing less well. In December there was shooting at Eastnor Castle and Coutts was there alone. In April Blanche was staying at Lockinge with Bob and Harriet; Coutts was at Eastnor. But in May husband and wife had taken a small house at Farnborough, close to Aldershot, where Coutts was being instructed in the new drill for the Volunteers. The house was surrounded by dark and shady fir trees, an oasis in the midst of camp with its all-permeating dust, Blanche remembered. And on 18 October at Cromwell Place a second child was born: a second daughter, Helen Anne, who was christened in December in the Oak Room at Balcarres. Just ten months later a third son, again illegitimate, fathered by Coutts, was born at 21 Bolsover Street, London, a street of fishmongers, bakers, asses'-milk dealers, mantua and straw-hat makers.

In later years this newcomer to Coutts's line would call himself James Lindsay but when his mother, Kate Madley, registered his birth it was as Arthur Harris Burfield Madley. The occupation of his (so-called) father, Henry Madley, was given as 'compositor'. Burfield had been the mother's maiden name and she has figured earlier in this story. In 1869 she was nineteen years of age. It is probable that she was a model which made it easier for her to account for the boy as, ostensibly, a child of a friend, a model, who had died after childbirth, leaving him in her care. Furthermore, No. 21 was situated at that end of Bolsover Street adjacent to Clipstone Street, once the site of the Clipstone Street Artist's Society, the haunt of artists working from the life, and where models still had lodgings. It is unlikely that there was any kind of marriage between Henry Madley and Kate Burfield, no marriage certificate exists, nor do they appear in any directory. By 1871 the lodging house in Bolsover Street was inhabited by a groom, a cab driver, and a porter, while Kate's mother, Mrs Harriet Burfield, a stay-maker, was domiciled in Great Portland Street in 1870. Who Henry Madley was is not known; his only appearance, and that bureaucratic, was to give the child a name on a birth certificate in the sub-district of All Souls Church and the registration district of Marylebone.

24
Tensions and Diversions

The impression Coutts had left on Lionel de Rothschild in 1869 was that he had 'grown into an old man' and was 'fearfully altered' since they had last met in 1865. The portrait taken in about that year by the photographer Wilkie Wynfield, showing Coutts dressed in shining armour,[34] and again that taken by his pupil Julia Cameron, are both of a man in his early forties but seemingly older. The silver-grey hair swept carelessly back from a broad forehead is at odds with his still dark and rather shaggy moustache. The small eyes are deep set but very observant and the features, owing perhaps to the lack of side-whiskers and the all-enveloping beard of the period, appear uncommonly prominent although handsomely cast. His attire marks him as a 'Bohemian'. The countenance is neither happy nor serene yet his fascination is indubitable. Even Aunt Charlotte, though not caring much for him, admitted his compelling charm. Constance de Rothschild thought she would be frightened of him but found him all that was delightful. His attraction for women was immense: the quiet but forceful manner, the face lighting up attractively with a smile; a man dedicated to the arts, preferring the small intimate gathering to the ballroom. His gift of concentrating, with all his power to attract, on the woman with whom he was conversing gave him an appeal few could resist.

Blanche, meanwhile, by the end of the sixties had become heavy of figure, high-spirited still but making herself ridiculous in the eyes of a critical niece who decided 'it was silly to send for Sir Coutts to carry her buxom rotundity swathed in green velvet and green braid à la Titian – in his arms upstairs.' Those portraits made of her now and in the next years show no vestige of the youthful face alive with the little suppressed smile glimpsed in one of the honeymoon photographs.

Her husband exhibited his two portraits of her at the Royal Academy in 1868 and 1870. The earlier of the two was perhaps the one made at Balcarres seated in the bow window. Her violin lies beside her and a brilliantly coloured cockatoo – the desire of a lifetime – has settled on her lap. Her head looks away into the garden and being in profile gives little indication of the mood of the sitter.[35] In the representation by the amateur artist Joseph Middleton Jopling, husband of her friend Louise Jopling, a professional portrait painter, Blanche is again seated with her violin at Balcarres, looking straight at the spectator. If there is anything to read in an otherwise expressionless face, it is perhaps a hint of sadness. Her portrait by G. F. Watts in the act of playing the violin in a room in Cromwell Place is a more lively piece of portraiture and denotes her musical progress, for she had given herself up almost entirely to the violin since having had to submit to all the annoyance and anxiety caused by the weakness of her eyes. Harriet spoke of Blanche's beautiful playing; by 1875 she was accompanying Joachim at Aston Clinton in Spohr's *Bacarolle*.

There were certain tensions within the family too. It was Anne, Coutts's mother, who quite unconsciously prompted Blanche's acts of possessiveness. Anne was in Florence and Minnie, writing to her in May 1872, told of Coutts having had 'one or two regular "blow ups" with Blanche as she will keep him so absolutely away from his own people'. He had come to the determination to stand it no longer and 'to take his own way' by which he hoped to gain a little improvement. 'He spoke very bitterly. I never heard him do so before.' If he were ill he felt he would have no one but Blanche to see and that all his family would be kept away entirely.

Minnie was fond of Blanche who was always so cordial and glad to see her. She was eager to make allowances.

I am so sorry for her [she wrote], I feel that she began by being badly taught at home and having such a jealous and engrossing mother who never allowed her to make friends. She is devoted to Coutts and he would be quite happy but there is always on his mind a sense of injury in being prevented any freedom of action. She had a difficult part to play at first to gain her husband to herself; our part is to try and love Blanche and bring him nearer along with her.

Since Coutts still regarded Balcarres as his mother's natural home – as did Anne herself – the consequences are predictable. Blanche displayed jealousy even of Coutts caring for his own daughters. These lived in the nursery on the top floor with a French governess and were made to have baths in sea water brought up in casks from Colinsburgh. When the weather was cold they broke the ice in their jugs to wash in the morning. On a visit to Balcarres, Constance's mother remarked on the improvement to the quiet and somewhat subdued tone of the house when two bright little boys with their hearty laughter came to stay. But there is little mention of Effie and Helen except in the late summer of 1872 when Coutts was anxious to leave his children with Anne and not alone at Balcarres when he and Blanche went abroad.

The impression that Balcarres offered a climate of measured calm is not in tune with recollections of others. To enliven and divert with charades, amateur recitals and 'little drawing room pieces' (one such, a *Comédie du Salon*, written by Blanche herself) was the prevailing fashion at house parties, and Balcarres had its share. At Cromwell Place and in Scotland Blanche entertained excessively, choosing from what was known as 'Bohemian' or 'artistic' society, mostly ignoring if not ridiculing the 'aesthetic movement' now emerging, to be mocked for its pretentious appreciation of 'the beautiful' and 'good taste'. For this Blanche had little sympathy, it was a craze which 'I for one did not appreciate,' she had said. Coutts, who carried not an ounce of affectation in him but cared deeply for the art he practised with only moderate success, disliked the humbug and attitudinizing of the 'aesthetes', though with the opening of the Grosvenor Gallery in which Burne-Jones held pride of place – the admired favourite of these new enthusiasts – Coutts might have seemed guilty of compliance.

In 1871 he had contributed a long and successful discourse on 'Painting in Oil' in connection with the Fine Arts Division of the London International Exhibition. Picking out artists who had had an influence on the progress of the English School of Painting, he named Hogarth amongst others, for his particular treatment of human life; Landseer as the first to master animal form; Reynolds the most lasting influence of all. In the contemporary English School of Painting he referred to Millais, Noel Paton, Lewis, Sant, and Goodall. The increasing influence of the Ideal School of Art was typified by Watts and Leighton.

Coutts spoke of the want of systematic early training among students, and general defective education. 'A fostering hand is urgently required,' he said and urged those artists who had attained complete knowledge of their profession to devote some part of their time to such pupils as might ask for guidance. He wished also to be emphatic on the right use of models: no portrait of a model should be introduced into a work of imagination, nor should a sitter become a mere model to a portrait painter; in the first case, the conception of the artist should predominate, in the latter, the subject should dominate the artist.

Blanche had now a circle of friends who would come

willingly to Balcarres and enjoy the company of their gifted hosts and the lion of the moment. Dicky Doyle, humorous but shy, would recall how his shortage of wardrobe embarrassed him so deeply when he stayed with the Lindsays that he would lock his clothes in a drawer at night and in the morning watch the wild despair of the footman searching for the secreted garments so as to attend to them.[36]

Blanche was often at Aston Clinton in 1873 painting Constance's portrait, who thought she had real talent and was 'curiously interesting' and 'a nice dear creature'. She recorded a beautiful day's hunting with Coutts, her horse carrying her to perfection. The cousins got on well together, sharing a love of music, though occasionally the atmosphere was slightly ruffled as when, for instance, Blanche was busy sending out invitations for a musical evening at Cromwell Place and Constance 'spent the greater part of the morning with Blanche who was busy with her invitations and quite full of that one subject and that one subject only'. Constance was a conscientious philanthropist who took infinite pains with her charitable work and succeeded in establishing a position for herself, so that Blanche, who had no such interests, and whose 'life seems small and purposeless', wearied her cousin 'to death'.

A invitation to Balcarres in September 1873 had brought Constance to Edinburgh to lay in what she called 'an immense store of winter things' in readiness for the pouring rain and piercing wind which she feared to meet and was obliged to endure. Edith Story and her brother were also guests. Coutts had known their father William Wetmore Story, the American sculptor, in Rome a good many years before. One day there had been an expedition to St Andrews: Constance had driven in a phaeton with Blanche and had felt nervous and anxious all the way. Yet, though bitterly cold, she claimed to have enjoyed herself there though she had more than cause to feel nervous again on the return journey when the horses bolted. Coutts was at hand and what might have ended in worse than tears was quickly resolved. The next day Constance reported cheerfully that 'Sir Coutts was wonderfully cool and collected' and the horses all right after their escapade.

25

A Preliminary Step

At Balcarres in 1874 a new star was prominent. This was the composer Arthur Sullivan, probably first encountered the previous year at a Mentmore house party. He was already a celebrity, ambitious, and immensely popular, with a deep fund of gaiety, and Blanche found his company entrancing. Annie Yorke, Constance's younger married sister, was not over-impressed. 'Sullivan, a very nice little man when one has seen more of him and has got over the eccentricities of his appearance; he is full of fun.' That summer, having floated down the Moselle from Treves to Coblenz, the Lindsays had travelled to meet him and a pleasant party of friends at Dresden – where Blanche set up her easel and made a copy of the *Holy Family* by Palma Vecchio and of Raphael's *Sistine Madonna*.

Almost at once on their return a house party was assembled at Balcarres. Sullivan was there as well as new friends, the Joplings, to entertain. Joseph Middleton Jopling, a self-trained artist and friend of Millais, had married Louise Romer this year, his first marriage, her second. Louise Jopling was a professional artist, had studied in Paris and had had some success in portrait painting. Her straitened means obliged her to work hard, to seek commissions and to keep a beady eye on the main chance; her determination was to succeed; her tendency to self-praise was perhaps muted when in company with the Lindsays, and she readily joined in any amusement. The part she played in the Lindsay ménage is an equivocal one: she appealed to Blanche as being a woman ready for a 'lark' and living by her own skills. To Coutts she also appealed, and

she found him one of the handsomest men she had ever
seen and in conversation extremely fascinating. She
summed up Blanche as a kind of Admirable Crichton, who
painted well, played the violin extremely well, and had a
talent for writing short stories, drawing-room plays and
verse. 'Blanche Lady Lindsay when I first saw her [she
wrote] was a very attractive looking woman, with hair of a
rich brown colouring and beautiful blue eyes. She was very
clever and very witty, but as I used to laugh and tell her,
her chief delight was to appear foolish.[37] During these
weeks J. M. Jopling made a portrait of Blanche. Nine
months later a boy was born to Louise, christened Lindsay
Millais, to whom John Millais stood godfather. Annie
Yorke was frank in her summing up of the Joplings: 'I do
not care much about him, I think he is tiresome, conceited
and silly; Mrs Jopling is a nice, clever, *entrain* little
woman.'

George Goschen M.P., then First Lord of the Admiralty,
and his wife, were also of the party and at their departure
he wrote Blanche a message in verse* from a country
platform during an hour's wait for the train. Based on one
of Sullivan's most popular of songs, 'Looking Back', there
were pertinent allusions to matters that had amused them
all during their stay: the 'aesthetes', Louise Jopling the
artist, also as a model for Blanche's brush, the 'nine-
pounder' melon likened to a naval cannon-ball[38] – and
others. Blanche's reply had likewise been in verse.

It was not only in Scotland that Blanche entertained. At
Cromwell Place friends from Coutts's youth were not
forgotten. Mrs Grote, elderly and stout, in a flounced dress
of fawn-coloured stuff, so short that it showed her black
kid shoes and the 'black ribbons of which were crossed
over her ankles neatly cased in white stockings' – at a time
when others wore trains even out of doors. Lady Eastlake,
a widow now, soberly dressed and her hair worn wound

*Appendix I

round her ears in little plaits secured by small gold pins. Mrs Sartoris was one who recognized Blanche's intelligence. There had been no check to her quick and sarcastic manner, her sense of humour was as lively as ever. She recounted how when walking in Paris she had paused to look in an old curiosity shop window and had been accosted by a loiterer, perhaps attracted by the youthfulness of her figure since her back was turned to him, who addressed her: 'Madame aime les antiquités?' Mrs Sartoris at no loss for words, veered round, threw back her veil: 'Monsieur aussi, apparement.' She was a capital croquet player and they played regularly at Balcarres. At another time with Leighton, the Hallés and Val Prinsep as fellow guests, she entered into all the fun of a charade in which Val Prinsep acted out the word in a 'blue beard' and red turban. Mrs Alma-Tadema, obliged to dress in a mode to comply with the spirit of her husband's paintings, would wear a severely classical robe, sandals, and a large gold serpent bracelet a little below the shoulder; her reddish hair was combed low upon her forehead. Blanche's own apparel was questioned by her cousin Annie Yorke at a dinner where she was dressed 'in demi-picturesque' and behaved in a rather silly and giggly manner – as always when with Madame Neruda (the fine violinist, later Lady Hallé), 'full of little jokes which nobody understood and nobody laughed at but herself'. Not suprisingly, in December of that year, 1874, when the Lindsays had stayed at Aston Clinton, Blanche had seemed to Constance weak and tired after so much social turmoil. 'No shooting,' she reported laconically, 'a kind of general lolling about.'

Encompassed by impedimenta for painting, easels, folding stools and umbrellas, the Lindsays when they travelled abroad had once been taken for acrobats at an Italian custom-house. In August 1875, similarly inelegant, they had set out for Cadennabia on Lake Maggiore reinforced with all the equipment of artists and with Arthur Sullivan himself. The heat was excessive; they saw only the cellist

Piatti, and wandered in the gardens of the absent Duke of Meiningen, enjoying his tall magnolias and the lemon trees in fruit. All this Blanche recounted in a letter[39] to Sullivan's mother, to whom he was very close.

That autumn, having presumably discussed the matter with Sullivan, Coutts had started to write words for an opera to be called 'Mary Stuart' when he received a finished libretto from Sullivan for the same purpose. That brought the project to a close – as with so many of Coutts's endeavours – but a year later Blanche herself had launched into composition.

There had been a great storm off the Fife coast at St Monan's, within a mile or two of Colinsburgh, with much loss of life. Blanche had held a charity bazaar in the village school to raise money for the widows and orphans of the fishermen. She had sold fifteen of her own drawings and had commissions for a further nine. Constance's mother had sent ten pounds for drawings and Blanche wondered how they could deal with all the orders which the 'kind patronage of friends have brought down on our devoted heads'. Besides which, she had composed a song, 'Fishermen of St Monan's', and had turned to Sullivan for guidance in getting it published. He was in Glasgow – the Lindsays at Balcarres – where he was leading the Glasgow Choral and Orchestral Union for two months. From the Hanover Hotel he wrote to Blanche on 17 December 1875 asking for the proofs which he would see through the press. She was to sign each copy 'B.L.' before any publisher sold them. 'Let the song be priced 4/– as it will sell for 2.' He was being so hard worked at concerts and rehearsals that he doubted whether he would get to Balcarres for the 'merrie Christmas-tide'.[40] In fact he did, and exclaimed enthusiastically of the view of the Firth of Forth from his window, seemingly divine with the co-mingling of the sun, first red, then white, making it look like a gold and silver sea alternately. They had had a tree on Christmas afternoon for the servants (no mention of Effie and Helen joining in) and he and Coutts had had a long walk on the seashore. They may have been discussing an enterprise that Coutts had been considering for some few years past and with which his name will always be joined.

On 20 March 1872, at the South Kensington Museum lecture theatre, Coutts had distributed prizes of medals and books to students of the South Kensington District School of Art, won in the National Competition of 1871. This he had followed with an address in which he had observed that the education in industrial artistic design from English schools had greatly prospered and that he now urged amongst other matters that the sculptor's art, which so far had been confined to modelling in clay, might master the working of stone, marble, and metal chasing. He drew attention to the lack of drapery study which was of first importance to the sculptor and the artist; that the education of a painter was one which could never be closed. The address was frequently interrupted by the applause of a crowded audience and was noticed in the press.

This had so irritated the old hands at the Royal Academy, who objected to his having trespassed on their own home ground, that when next month Coutts had sent in a picture for that summer's exhibition, it had been rejected. Millais, who was staying at the time with the Holfords at Westonbirt, was incensed, remembering no doubt how nearly twenty-five years earlier he and two others had raised the Pre-Raphaelite banner in opposition to the Royal Academicians and their followers. Since 1862 Coutts had had eight pictures at the Royal Academy exhibitions but many excellent artists had not been given space and canvases had been carelessly hung. This had given rise to dissatisfaction and some latent murmurings. To circumvent this opposition Coutts envisaged hiring a gallery for one exhibition only. When this proved impossible a more ambitious idea had germinated: this was to build a gallery himself to which he would invite such artists as he wanted.

The year 1876 brought the first part of this venture to fruition. There was much planning and discussing, carried on for the greater part at Balcarres or in London where in March the guests at dinner were J. Comyns Carr, critic on the staff of the *Pall Mall Gazette*, where he had written on Royal Academy reform; Charles Hallé, mediocre artist, and son of the distinguished musician; and the George Howards. They had just returned from three months in Rome where George had sketched in the *campagna* while dreaming of a school of painting which he and others would eventually form. Also there was Louise Jopling, much in favour of the new enterprise, and equally in favour with the Lindsays. Separated temporarily from her husband, who was in America, she advised him that she had 'told Sir Coutts that if I got into any mischief during your absence it would be his fault, if he did not look after me properly'. That same month she had twice accompanied the Lindsays, once to the opera where Rothschild cousins had given Blanche their box for *La Favorita*, and where 'the constant Arthur Sullivan dropped in', and to the Peoples' Concert at Battersea where Blanche's song, 'Fishermen of St Monan's' was included in the programme; this 'went off very well'.[41] The Loyd-Lindsays were there, Colonel Lindsay and his daughter Violet (later Duchess of Rutland), and Tom Taylor.

Abroad in the early summer, the Lindsays were in France, mostly in Paris, at Fontainebleau, and at St Germain-en-Laye where after dinner on a June evening Blanche and Coutts walked on the terrace with Constance, whose father had recently died. They were home in time to be honoured by the presence of Princess Louise at lunch at Cromwell Place, a honour which prevented Coutts from attending a meeting of the board of Trustees of the National Portrait Gallery.[42]

August saw the Lindsays and Sullivan in the west Highlands and by October a large house party had gathered at Balcarres. Annie Yorke found the air deliciously bracing though the weather was 'decidedly Scotch'. It had rained nearly every day, but having revised her opinion of Sullivan, she managed a nine-mile walk with him. Louise Jopling was highly entertained 'by the days so delightfully filled up', and Blanche had undertaken to write a one-act play about three fisher girls, and she, Louise, would wear appropriate costume and a Brittany cap. Blanche had been studying harmony and counterpoint with Sullivan for the last two years and in spite of his being 'dreadfully critical' they had had a fair amount of music, not necessarily entirely welcome to Sullivan. For to one who was always late for breakfast it could not have been of vast amusement to be wakened by his hostess and the Swedish singer, Christine Nilsson, who with two violins played Braga's *Serenata*, an entertainment piece, outside his bedroom door, knowing as they did how weary he was of hearing it.

Christine Nilsson had cut an amazing figure later in the day. Having insisted on going shooting with the men, she had equipped herself with high Russian boots and a short black leather skirt topped by a tight cloth jacket, while on her fair hair perched a Tyrolean hat. Her skill at shooting was not apparent: an unsuspecting rabbit had been blown to pieces at the distance of three yards. Such conduct could not have appealed to Coutts, nor to his mother – present this rare occasion. Indeed, as reported Annie Yorke, Blanche also seemed not to get on very well 'with Mrs Lindsay, or rather they seem perfectly indifferent to each other. Blanche is to my mind a little wanting in attention and Mrs Lindsay in affection. Sir Coutts, on the contrary, is perfectly devoted to his mother; she is a very clever woman and I should think he enjoys her society extremely' – in contrast, one might say, to his wife's antics and those of the Swedish singer.

Perhaps he was not unduly irritated, though for some time past he had been aware that Blanche seldom invited members of his family to Balcarres – perhaps it was in retaliation for his infidelities – but he was much engaged with plans for the new gallery and having taken a momentous step, the immediate future depended on decisive actions. With the support of Charles Hallé and Comyns Carr, his wife's money and the good will of many, Coutts was in a justifiably prominent, and agreeable, position. The year closed with the Joplings sharing Christmas Day at Cromwell Place and 1877 was ushered in with an acceleration of building and a wave of enthusiasm.

26
The Building of the Grosvenor Gallery

When the Grosvenor Gallery opened its doors to the public on 1 May 1877 at 135 New Bond Street, the first to arrive was Whistler (seven of his works were being shown); G. F. Watts in a long sealskin coat, perhaps feeling the chill of an early May morning, was the next to follow and Browning, Henry James, Augustus Sala, Oscar Wilde, and many more in succession. Friends of the Lindsays from the political, artistocratic and art world accounted for part of the 7,000 who had crowded the rooms to admire or criticize. When the doors closed that evening the vindication of over eighteen anxious months of intensive activity seemed assured.

The site for the Gallery building[43] was a fair-sized piece of ground in Grosvenor Mews, on the Grosvenor estate, running north and south between Grosvenor Street and Brook Street, containing a hybrid assortment of stabling and sheds. The main entrance, fronting on to New Bond Street, was on ground belonging to the Corporation of the City of London. William Sams, the chosen, though generally unknown, architect, responded to Coutts's desire for a building resembling in character a Renaissance palace; this same theme was to be carried through into the galleries themselves. The foundations had been laid in 1876 and as the building progressed, rising to four storeys above the ground floor, Coutts received daily injunctions for loss of Ancient Lights (air and light). So as to avoid further trouble and to ensure space, he had been obliged to buy two of the neighbouring houses, allowing him a good frontage for a shop on either side.

The marble centrepiece in New Bond Street was the Palladian doorway, flanked on either side by two Corinthian columns, said to have been by the master himself. Rescued by George Cavendish-Bentinck at the time of the demolition of the Venetian church of Santa Lucia,[44] it was acquired from him by Coutts. Above rose an ornate three-bay building in Portland stone, the windows dissected by pilasters.

Inside, from the great vestibule, rich with green Genoese marble columns, there rose an imposing staircase carrying pedestals in niches for statues to the first floor, passing the smaller sculpture and watercolour rooms on the way. At the head of the stairs the entry to the west and principal gallery leading from the east gallery, the smaller of the two, was a moment of exquisite astonishment. Here was a lofty ceiling of cerulean blue sprinkled with stars copied from Coutts's studio in Cromwell Place which directed the eye to Whistler's work of the phases of the moon on the coving below, the two separated by Coutts's frieze displaying an ebullience of garlanded *putti* ingeniously hiding a form of ventilation. Crimson silk damask covered the wall spaces; these were intersected by sixteen gilded cream-coloured pilasters recovered from the old Italian opera house in Paris. In contrast, the dado was draped in dark green velvet extending to the parquet floor, itself requiring attention for fear the tone might work to the disadvantage of the surrounding brilliance. Such splendour was not confined to the walls; velvet sofas and gilded-wood tables, some inlaid with marbles, were discreetly placed. Flowers and exotic plants had come from Mentmore, Westonbirt, from the Crawfords, and from the Loyd-Lindsays at Lockinge.

A restaurant, a component part of the plan, was situated beneath the galleries; this too was decorated in style. Gilt Ionic columns on each side of the room divided it into spaces with tables which could be enclosed by draperies or screens for further privacy. The kitchen and general offices were, according to the *Illustrated London News*, 'replete with every requisite'. A lessee for the restaurant had not yet been secured and this had given Coutts the extra work of getting it started as well as having to dispense with the rent.

By transforming his gallery into what more than one voice likened to the house of some patrician, or 'a Medici', he and Blanche (for its creation was partly hers) had established premises not as rivals to the Royal Academy, but where by invitation artists could show such paintings as they themselves had selected; each man's work would be grouped by itself in the amount of space he expected to fill, and with no overcrowding. Originally Coutts had entertained a scheme of combining music with painting but this had been too difficult to effect.

When the project had been still in embryo he had propounded that exhibitors were not to include artists from the Royal Academy, but this point had been dropped so as not to antagonize Burlington House. Certain members had been invited from there, including their President, Sir Francis Grant, who had written cordially to Coutts, having always 'encouraged a large and liberal spirit, avoiding all mean jealousies'. He was happy to contribute a picture and would endeavour to send one of his best. Coutts had definite ideas whom he would invite to this first exhibition but he had not reckoned with the perversity of two outstanding artists, Ford Madox Brown, touchy and generally on the look-out for slights, who had refused to cooperate as he had not been consulted among the first, and D. G. Rossetti on professional grounds, since he never exhibited anywhere, being sensitive to criticism; also he felt that this revised procedure of including Royal Academy artists was incompatible with the existence of the Grosvenor Gallery.

Hallé and Coutts had gone round to many of the studios, sometimes on horseback, and had helped in the selection of a number of exhibits. Once the subject and dimensions of the work had been obtained it was cut out to scale on cardboard and attached to a mock-up of the gallery walls, tones of colour being carefully contrasted.

In all some one hundred and fifty works were on the walls for the Private View on 30 April and the public opening on 1 May. One shilling entrance fee and no vulgar red dots to indicate the sale of a picture. Whistler's image of Carlyle dominated the turnstiles and may have been hung there as a jest, being assured of the sitter's rooted dislike of art.

During all these months Blanche had enthusiastically backed her husband and had agreed to forgo the improvement of a new hall at Balcarres and other alterations. Together, in about equal shares, they had financed the venture, approximated at £120,000. Though still in her early thirties her health was not robust and her figure, no longer youthful, overweight. She had been saddened in the spring, grieving over the death of her parrot, but during the weeks preparatory to the Gallery's opening she had struggled to help. Coutts, writing out to his mother at the Villa Palmieri in Florence, had assured her that Blanche had been 'so good and helpful, but she is and has been so unwell from cold and weakness and she is unfit for anything'.

Poor Blanchy; she had not only her health to contend with but also Coutts's offensive behaviour, in moral terms, to tolerate. It is natural to suppose that she knew of the two sons fathered in his youth, but Kate Madley had never faltered in her devotion and was still integral to Coutts's life. Of this Blanche was very much aware.

The days before the opening were charged with worries: the chief difficulty lay in securing the promised works from artists who had pleaded for grace to complete them. Coutts had further trouble. He had been obliged, by the Prince of Wales's request, to accept a place on the committee for the next Paris International Exhibition; this had been impossible to refuse as the Prince had supported him over the formation of the gallery and was honouring the Lindsays at dinner there on 9 May. 'My darling Mum,' Coutts wrote out to Florence, 'to say the truth although I am full of fight I am getting tired of the struggle. I sometimes wish I could shut myself away from everyone.' He praised Hallé who had worked 'day and night in the cause'; all the staff had been indefatigable, establishing an *esprit de corps* throughout, achieving what nothing else would have accomplished.

On the evening before the opening when all seemed in place, it was discovered that gas had not been laid on in the watercolour room. What might have been disaster was saved by the Lindsays' carriage driving back and forth between Cromwell Place and New Bond Street carrying all the gas lamps that could be mustered. At last Blanche, Coutts, Comyns Carr, and Charles Hallé sat down at one in the morning to a picnic supper in the large gallery and drank to the success of the new exhibition.

27

The Grosvenor Gallery

A success it undoubtedly was. Fashion thronged the rooms, amazed at the splendour, the space, the lighting, and the attraction of the pictures. But not all was admired. Much of the public was antagonistic, supported in part by professional critics who were ill-disposed towards the works on show; these exhibited 'a lack of morality', were 'unmanly', and breathed unwholesome 'morbidness' and 'decadence'. But the effect achieved by his gallery and the magnificence within was what Coutts, with his love for the *quattrocento*, had aimed at; it was not a manifestation of W. S. Gilbert's later allusion in the opera *Patience* to a 'Greenery-yallery Grosvenor Gallery', nor could Coutts have been recognized as 'a foot in the grave young man'.

However, before long the cult of aestheticism had become synonymous with the influence generated by the Grosvenor Gallery, informed largely by the works of Edward Burne-Jones, evoking what Henry James disparagingly termed 'an aesthetic refinement' based on the painter's esoteric compositions and the wearied androgynous figures that filled his canvas – poses which the fashionable quickly adopted and which gave George Du Maurier the perfect target for his satirically aesthetic cartoons in *Punch*.[45]

The innovation of the hanging (each man to his own wall space and nothing skied) was sound, but in a few cases the crimson damask was near-disaster. To Holman Hunt's *Afterglow in Egypt* it was calamitous. To Burne-Jones, who carried the day with his magical canvases, the crimson was anathema. He had realized this would be so almost from the start, but as a friend of Coutts and a man of great modesty, he had not wished to interfere. Also the accessories of tables, objects, and sofas reflected in the glasses of his paintings. Nevertheless, this opportunity to show his pictures (he had exhibited very little since 1871) enhanced his reputation and brought him to the forefront, justifying Rossetti's opinion that his name represented 'the loveliest art we have'.

Whistler fared better; for him the hangings were a foil to his greys and misty blue-blacks, though his *Nocturnes* were a bewilderment to many.[46] Ruskin, who was in Venice at the time of the opening of the gallery, made his visit on 23 June (a day of 'old black evil sky') and dined in the evening with the Burne-Joneses to whom he was devoted. His condemnation was directed at Coutts, 'an amateur both in art and shop-keeping', who with a desire to manage the gallery rightly, 'must not put his own works in it until he can answer for their quality; if he means to be a painter, he must not at present superintend the erection of public buildings, or amuse himself with their decoration by china and upholstery.' He berated the upholstery in particular, for 'its glitter as unjustly veils the vulgarity of the worst'. And for Whistler's paintings he had nothing but contempt and no understanding. He upbraided Coutts for admitting works into his gallery 'in which the ill-educated conceit of the artist so nearly approached the aspect of wilful imposture'.

His attack on one particular painting, Whistler's *Nocturne in Black and Gold: the Falling Rocket* was thought by the artist to be libellous. 'I have seen, and heard, much of Cockney impudence before now [Ruskin wrote in *Fors Clavigera*]; but never expected to hear a coxcomb ask two hundred guineas for flinging a pot of paint in the public's face.'[47] Whistler promptly sued him; the law suit was heard the following year when Whistler was awarded one farthing damages and obliged to pay his costs and went bankrupt. The gallery gained wide publicity.

At the opening Blanche's works understandably hung in a central position and Coutts thought that his own, seven in number, looked better here than they would anywhere excepting a private house. The *Art Journal* considered his portrait of his wife was 'much sweeter and truer' than Watts's portrayal of Blanche with violin where 'what gives character to the countenance has here failed'.

The Somerses' eldest daughter, Isabel, had married Lord Henry Somerset, who in writing to his mother-in-law exclaimed: 'You can't fancy anything more satisfactory and beautiful than the Grosvenor Gallery and its *divine* pictures. Sir Coutts was nice and warm in his welcome. I can't say Lady Lindsay *was* particularly cordial or civil, but then we all know what an idiot she is.'[48] Lord Henry, whose scandalous homosexual behaviour would force him in the near future to live abroad, had readily adopted what had perhaps always been Virginia's opinion.

To Anne, May was able to report on the evening of the opening day that the rooms looked very handsome. 'Many pictures I do not care about and some that I admire very much. Coutts says that it has been a great success. He looks so happy and relieved and well and is not overtired.'

Ten days later both he and Blanche had every reason to drop with fatigue. The Prince of Wales signified his readiness to dine at the Grosvenor Gallery and the restaurant was duly prepared for the occasion. The gardens of Gunnersbury, Mentmore once again, and even Balcarres provided a bank of flowers. There were to be one hundred and fifty guests and these included Princess Louise, Prince Leopold, Prince Arthur, and Princess Mary of Teck. Personal friends made up the number. The Lindsays' French chef, Gounard, and the other servants prepared everything. Plate was lent by Messrs Hancock, and Garrard. There had been heart-burning and little jealousies, particularly among the artists' wives, and conniving for invitations by others. As early as April Lord Henry Somerset had written to

Virginia of his surprise that Lord Tavistock (later Duke of Bedford) and 'Addy' his wife (Isabel's sister, Adeline) had not been invited. 'I should have thought Sir Coutts would have asked them, but perhaps Lady Lindsay is jealous of her looks or position.'

Blanche remained late at New Bond Street overseeing the preparations and on arrival home there was little time allowed for changing into her elaborate dress; no time to put on her jewels, so these she had simply bundled into her lap, managing to bedeck herself in the carriage on her way back to the Gallery where a crisis had arisen.

It had been left to Sullivan and Hallé to fix the seating at table and to pair off the couples as they were 'armed' down to dinner, but the number of guests, mostly arriving together, disorganized such arrangements as had existed. It was providential that the Prince and his entourage were assembled at table in their correct places.

'The Grosvenor Gallery dinner was a great success last night,' wrote Lord Henry on 10 May. 'Everything was wonderfully well done. There was I should think about a hundred and fifty at dinner, which was at several large tables with Sir Coutts and some of the Royalties and particular swells at the top end and Lady Lindsay and some more Royalties at the bottom. The dinner itself was very good, really wonderful considering the number that had to be fed, and altogether it was in every way *well* done.' After the banquet there was a reception for some five hundred people in the rooms above and Blanche carried off her position as hostess with flying colours. With her undoubted flair for entertaining she held Sunday afternoon tea parties ('splendid convocations'[49]) in the gallery's restaurant, mingling art world with society. The Princess of Wales with her children occasionally attended, plunging into the irresistible homemade chocolate cake.

28
A Royal Visit

The Summer Exhibition had closed at the beginning of August and the Lindsays hurried north to breathe fresh air and recruit from the exigencies of a restless summer. They were at Palace House, Beaulieu staying with the Montagus, when news came that Prince Leopold, the Queen's youngest (and haemophilic) son intended to visit them at Balcarres. This plan had perhaps been initiated by Princess Louise, his devoted sister, herself closely acquainted with Blanche (whose portrait of her would be hung at the Grosvenor Gallery the next year). She had dined with the Lindsays in London that summer and knowing how much Leopold resented Queen Victoria's strict management of his life, owing in particular to the circumstances of his health, may have thought that a visit to Balcarres might offer him a sensation of freedom. The idea might even have been instigated by Blanche, who by entertaining royalty would place herself on a level with various of her Rothschild relations.

A house party was hastily assembled to welcome the young Prince: Dicky Doyle was present, Arthur Sullivan and Mrs Ronalds his mistress, a Bostonian of beauty and wealth, and with, too, an appealing singing voice. Also Comyns Carr and his wife Alice who was generally thought to be the inspirer of Mrs Cimabue Brown, the archtypal aesthete of George Du Maurier's *Punch* cartoons. She designed and made dresses for the stage and counted herself a true Bohemian, finding many of her friends among theatre people, who in that class-conscious age were a remove lower than artists, musicians and writers. Consequently her shyness as a young married woman at Balcarres evoked little sympathy from Blanche. 'She lacked the gift of making her guests feel at home.' Blanche's acknowledged nickname for her was 'Feeble', which while spoken jokingly may not have found particular favour with Alice Carr who got her own back in later life when referring to Blanche: 'She always liked knowing artists and musicians, and herself dabbled in both these arts, though later the pen of an easy writer claimed her affections and she published much Society prose. But we of the Bohemian world were never deceived into thinking that she *really* included us in her "inner circle" of her own friends.'[50]

On 21 September 1877, the evening of the Prince's arrival, Coutts was at the railway station of Kilconquhar with a carriage and four and postilions. The moon was rising as Leopold emerged from his carriage and he was quickly driven the two miles to Balcarres. The visit was a fairly lengthy one but it gave opportunities for picnics, lawn tennis, and excursions into the countryside on which Blanche, in her phaeton drawn by two chestnuts, would invariably drive the Prince herself.[51]

Entertainment within doors was not so happy. Leopold was easy enough to amuse if he were sufficiently flattered, and flattery laid on with a trowel was the easy way to please. However, one evening when Sullivan, whose skills at the piano had been much in demand throughout the visit, retired to the smoking room for a cigar, Leopold had sent for him. He wanted to dance and Sullivan, exhausted and irritated, was to play. Sullivan's reply, spoken slowly, came very distinctly: 'You may tell him that I'll see him damned first.'[52] He was also probably aware, for it must have been an open secret amongst the guests, that Queen Victoria had expressed a strict order that there should be no dancing for fear of the Prince over-tiring himself, so that what with Leopold demanding to dance, and the perpetual pretence of being unable to move the heavy dining-room table out of the way to allow space enough, perhaps Sullivan's downright refusal, reworded into a tactfully evasive form, had helped his hosts out of an awkwardness.

Often they would gather around the piano which had been brought downstairs from the schoolroom while Sullivan played over music he was composing for his future opera, *The Sorcerer*, which would open in November. Blanche's song, 'Sometimes', set to music by Sullivan and published the same year, may have originated now, as also a piece of music Sullivan composed, 'I Would I Were a King', perhaps to make amends for his earlier behaviour, and dedicated 'by special desire' to the Prince and published in 1878.[53] Suffering from bad health, he often wrote his melodies in the London Library while stretched out on a sofa in great pain.[54] Now he was the entertainer-in-chief, but on the point of departure he suffered a violent haemorrhage and was obliged to remain still longer at Balcarres.

Theatricals were also in demand. Blanche enjoyed devising and acting in tableaux and with the assistance of the house guests and the abundant contribution of the Balcarres 'tableau chest', eight short sketches were performed in one evening, following an afternoon lawn tennis party. Tableau III, squeezed in between *Rebecca at the Well*, and *The Sultana*, was the principal attraction. For here was Blanche, dressed as Queen Henrietta Maria, kneeling before Charles I (Prince Leopold) bidding him an emotional farewell. For the fifth tableau Blanche had resuscitated her *Fishwives* (which Mrs Jopling had praised a year earlier in the chance of a Breton woman's cap) and had written a duet, 'Spin, Sisters, Spin', which she sang with Alice Carr to an admiring audience.

Sunday morning brought problems of another kind. It had been settled that the Prince would attend the Scotch Episcopal Church of St John's at Pittenweem where Coutts worshipped, but the Queen having become aware that this was intended instructed Leopold by telegram on Saturday night to attend a Scotch Presbyterian church. Plans were in disarray, the vicar of St John's had not been informed of the change of plan until ten o'clock on Sunday morning when a larger-than-usual congregation was already seen to be arriving. Mr Irvine on the other hand, the minister of the parish church at Kilconquhar, had only returned from Wales on Saturday and was apprised that night of the honour awaiting him. The church was sufficiently large to accommodate over a thousand people, but the attendance was on the meagre side since there had been no time to ensure a large turn-out. However, according to the *Fife News*, 'the august party' occupied the family pew and the distinguished appearance of the occupants ('more distinguished than has been accommodated in it for a long time') caused a considerable flutter in the congregation composed of agricultural folk, who for the most part conducted themselves with 'becoming propriety'. The service was of the usual simple Presbyterian order though the minister surely excelled himself by preaching 'a very good evangelical discourse' (*Fife News* again) 'on "The Son of Man shall come in his glory" ', taken from St Matthew's Gospel. Blanche had driven the Prince there and back.

Two days later Leopold took his departure. Meditating on the strangeness of having had none of his family or young relations at Balcarres for the visit – his wife preferring her own set of friends – Coutts had written despondently to his mother that he was suffering from a great depression of spirits and disinclination to do anything. 'I see very few of you all here now; I dont much care for the constant Society that we have here.' He had found Leopold much the least interesting of the brothers and certainly very feeble both in body and mind and acting more like a spoilt child than a man, but he was goodtempered and kind-hearted and he had perhaps enjoyed himself.

Before the autumn was out plans had been consolidated for the Winter Exhibition. This was to consist chiefly of Old Master drawings: Holbeins lent by the Queen, while at Chatsworth Dicky Doyle had found drawings by Raphael, Michelangelo and Leonardo hanging in dirty frames in passages 'and most unexpected places'.[55] These, and works from other notable collections, ensured the success of the enterprise.

For the Summer Exhibition of 1878 Blanche's portrait of Princess Louise would be much in evidence in the east gallery. As a result of a friendly attitude on the princess's part Blanche was enabled to include her close friends in her small lunch parties for her royal guest. Louise Jopling (or 'Pierrette' as she was known to Blanche) was an intimate at these gatherings, adding a professional element to balance that of the princess. Other contributors included Leighton, Millais, George Howard, Whistler with *Nocturnes* and his *Arrangement in Black* of Henry Irving as Philip II of Spain; Blanche had added her own *No More Hairpins*, one of several watercolours.

The early part of 1878 was not short of incident. Coutts had contrived to let both front shops in New Bond Street at good rentals but the constant watchfulness required was inimical to him and a heavy burden: 'being supposed a very rich man and an amateur in business, everyone connected with the venture thinks that he can act the generous part at my expense.' Also, the restaurant was not paying; this was a constant irritant and never wholly resolved, but at present he had hopes of letting it at £2,500 a year. He was also being driven into 'a very warm corner' and had to fight in self-defence for he had many hundred applications from artists to show their works in the coming exhibition and even the Prince of Wales, who was very touchy, and who could not well be refused having been one of Coutts's warmest supporters, had asked for a good many pictures to be shown. It seemed to Coutts that it was the indifferent work that was the most pushed.

In the spring Blanche was over-tired and, taking Mrs Jopling with her, escaped to a house near Christchurch in Hampshire, belonging to Lord Bury, a relation of Coutts. With the Prince of Wales and Arthur Sassoon she attended the wedding of her cousin Hannah Rothschild to Lord Primrose (later Lord Rosebery) at Mentmore. The bride had a cold but was in wonderful spirits and 'as little affected as possible', according to Aunt Charlotte (with perhaps a backward glance at Blanche's marriage).

Meanwhile another marriage was breaking up and with the greatest possible publicity. A legal separation had been finally established, but only through months of bitter fighting, after Isabel Somerset had threatened to bring to court Lord Henry, her homosexual husband, unless he agreed to a separation and to her having sole custody of the child, a son born in 1874 and now four years old. She did not wish for a divorce as it was against the law of the Church. Horror and astonishment predominated in society, not so much on account of the husband's criminal practices (and few women understood the nature of the offence), but because his wife – a woman – threatened to expose Lord Henry in an affidavit in such terms that it was past belief that any woman could put such things upon paper. Her examination in court would have been so fearful that it was incomprehensible how a modest woman would be able to bear it. The Somerses suffered much opprobrium for their influence on their daughter, Virginia in particular, who had added fuel to the flames by melodramatically stating that it were better her daughter should go over to the Church of Rome, where she would undoubtedly get an annulment, rather than tolerate a mere separation. 'All the old stories against Virginia are brought up again,' May Holford wrote to her mother, 'and people say "What can you expect from such a woman?"' May herself, while not taking Lord

Henry's side, admitted that were Isabel her child she would rather lose her by death than see her go through such an awful ordeal. The terms of the deed of separation were finally agreed upon and Isabel was to have sole charge and custody of her son until he was twenty-one. Lord Somers collapsed under the strain; ostracized by society Isabel turned to a life of philanthropy and teetotalism, and Lord Henry Somerset departed to live in Florence.

The previous year Constance de Rothschild had married the very handsome Cyril Flower, a man of wealth who had inherited the large estate of Battersea from his father. Marriage to an Italian nobleman had been forbidden her during her father's lifetime on grounds of faith, but with his death, and with her mother's consent, she was free to marry where she chose. Only contented with the very best – a 'magnifico' if ever there was one – Cyril Flower (later first Lord Battersea), with his great love of art, had furnished Surrey House, Marble Arch, on the corner of Edgware Road and Oxford Street, with pictures, statuary and fine furniture, constituting a meeting-place for writers, musicians and philanthropists, and later, as Liberal Member of Parliament (Brecon, and Luton) for his party gatherings. Aston Clinton was also their home and as a fine rider he loved to hunt in the Vale of Aylesbury. His originality of taste was apparent not only in his tendency to ostentatiously brightly-coloured clothes but, to his wife's chagrin for she adored him, to the company he was inclined to keep. A framed photograph in his sitting-room of his young valet in white flannels and cricket bat[56] did not augur too well, any more than Constance's diary entry: 'Cyril brought down [to Aston Clinton] two young men which was a disturbing influence.'

In August of 1878 the Flowers and the Coutts Lindsays were at Pontresina at the same time, while later in the year Blanche was at Aston Clinton where she proved a most unsociable guest, spending much of the time in bed.

Venice had claimed Coutts and his wife most years and until it was taken by Guggenheim for an antiquarian shop, they had lodged at the Palazzo Balbi where the dilapidated *salone*, seventy feet long, looked down on the bend of the Grand Canal. Rawdon Brown, an old man now, who had spent the greater part of his life in Venice calendaring the Venetian State Papers, had been well disposed towards them and had shown them treasures they would not otherwise have seen. Blanche recalled how once – perhaps on their way to the Lido which she had loved for its rough grass by the water's edge, 'like in far off Scotland' – Rawdon Brown had discoursed on the superlative beauty and advantage of the Venetian mode of rowing and how a friend of the Lindsays had dared to commend the orderly crew of an English 'eight oar'. 'Savages on a log, my dear Sir, savages on a log,' Brown had exclaimed reprovingly.

Soon after the opening of the 1879 Summer Exhibition at the Grosvenor Gallery Coutts and Blanche had gone to North Devon: Clovelly they had found 'quite lovely' but Ilfracombe, a resort for bathers and pleasure seekers, had been, in consequence, detestable. Coutts was satisfied with his own pictures at the Gallery (*Ariadne* and *A Knight and His Daughter*) and had been in communication with a dealer to whom he hoped to sell them. Two pieces of information he reported to his mother in this same letter: that he had attended the funeral of Blanche's uncle, Baron Lionel de Rothschild, who had died on 3 June and where it had needed sixty mourning coaches and hundreds of carriages to transport relatives and friends. 'Rather a melancholy farce' it had seemed, and there remained poor Aunt Charlotte who had not taken in her husband's death and whose mind was confused. (She survived him until 1884.) Neatly sandwiched between the Rothschild funeral and a word about his daughters, now ten and fourteen years old, and their new dancing mistress ('I think it will improve their carriage' was his laconic comment), appeared the news that

Coutts Lindsay Chambers (the second son of his liaison with Lizzie) had written from Point Galle, south of Colombo, and on reaching Brisbane had telegraphed his arrival.

29
Separation and Departure

There were straws in the wind but no positive indication that the Lindsays' marriage was in danger and the lack of harmony during these years was perhaps not generally apparent. Towards the close of 1878 Minnie and her husband (now the 25th Earl of Crawford since his father's death in 1869) had stayed at Balcarres on a visit. There had been a good deal of rearrangement of rooms and general improvements of which Minnie had written enthusiastically to her mother, also more sense of 'repose' in the house since she was last there as Blanche had left them alone more. But it was not a pleasant house to stay in owing to Blanche's restless nature. Of the two daughters Minnie did not know what to think. They were not unhappy but it was a negative happiness at best with Blanche anxious to show them off to advantage to herself, to have them talk French and to play the piano. When their governess apologized for their not having played as well as they could, Blanche remonstrated sharply in German to the effect that this would discourage them. The eldest girl, Effie, was growing decidedly pretty with a lovely-shaped face which lit up now and again; Helen possessed that all too familiar 'nice honest little face' with few pretensions to looks and Coutts never spoke to them or took the slightest notice of them.

Blanche's own upbringing had been a cosmopolitan one and although she spoke of Scotland with affection it was perhaps more the ancient name and the house and her position which appealed to her. Coutts had travelled and lived much abroad but his roots were firmly in his native land like generations of his line before him. Blanche on the other hand had never fitted into the Scottish way of life. Her possessiveness was undiminished towards Coutts and the children, and Anne was all too rarely invited to her old home. 'Unfolding qualities of the most exacting and adhesive nature respecting Coutts – not overwise perhaps but much to be sympathised with [wrote a cousin] – with the passing years she was for ever whipping him to heel and displaying jealousies even in respect of his caring for his own two little girls.' She was approaching her late thirties and Coutts nearing his sixties but there had been no child for Blanche since Helen's birth, followed so swiftly by that of the unacceptable Arthur Madley. Yet both parents must surely have wished for a male heir; Coutts with his strongly held love and responsibility for Balcarres, while to Blanche it would have meant the termination of a possibly aspiring, usurping, Arthur Madley, whose name at about this time had given place to 'James Lindsay'. Having no legitimate heir to carry on his name, Coutts may have wished to have had Kate's son, now more than eleven years old, to stay occasionally at Balcarres, which Blanche would naturally have violently opposed. To the younger generation, the Crawfords' children for instance, Coutts did not endear himself: his manner was suave with a touch of arrogance, and yet the charm of his conversation was irresistible and his knowledge always a delight. The resentment and dislike was largely felt on account of the pain and anxiety he brought to the 'beloved elders'.

The domestic contingent at Cromwell Place was numerous: a governess and a housekeeper, two lady's maids, three housemaids, a kitchen and a scullery maid, a butler, two footmen and a page, while the chef lived out. Blanche indeed had many friends, but her incessant entertaining, often on the pretentious side, especially with regard to royalty, was irksome to Coutts. The Prince and Princess of Wales were at the Grosvenor in 1879; a year later they were there again for a concert and after their departure a dance was got up, and which was voted 'the greatest fun' and Louise Jopling danced with Coutts. In January of 1880 Blanche was at Brighton where with Mrs Jopling's assistance she arranged a musical afternoon and played the violin. Watts and Alfred Sassoon were among the audience. Bidden to join a party at Ashridge with Lady Marian Alford, Blanche had advised Louise to make herself as attractive as possible 'to maintain the character of my Balcarres company'.[57] Leighton, Browning, the Poynters, Alma-Tademas, George Eliot and G. H. Lewis, she knew them all – some more as acquaintances than particular friends. As a young woman she had first seen Tennyson at Little Holland House and in her admiration had followed him and Sara Prinsep across the lawn when to her dismay his first words spoken in his deeply resonant voice were: 'Is there mutton for dinner?' Latterly he had complained to her that Ruskin had criticized him for saying that a crushed daisy blushes red, by which Tennyson had implied that it showed the underside of its petals when crushed – this Ruskin had called sentimental fallacy.[58]

At Holman Hunt's studio in March 1880 he welcomed her kindly, his yellowing beard streaming wildly, his hollow eyes full of fire, the face of an enthusiast. *The Fisherman*, a portrait of his son, Cyril, was at the Grosvenor that year and Blanche remarked on the plum-coloured velvet boating costume and magenta tie

In the summer Louise Jopling went to Balcarres and remained there until October for Blanche was seriously ill. The malady is not known but seems to have been a collapse, a general debility brought on by nervous tension and worry. Coutts was mostly in London, painting in the gallery where he found the best light he had ever worked under. He was determined to make a success of his large Dante subject *The Boat of Charon*, from the *Inferno*, Canto iii (at the Grosvenor in 1881) and thus enable him, as he said, to take the place he had so long been fighting for: as head of a great section of Art. Mrs Jopling was assiduous with her letters and he was 'not only her debtor in this but in a thousand ways besides'.[59] When he returned to Scotland he found his wife in the lowest of spirits and in poor health and in January 1881 Blanche admitted to having gone through much suffering and grief which had preyed upon her for a long time. This in its turn had brought on a weary illness which prevented her shaking off the sad thoughts that 'eat away my strength and sap my brain'.

The D'Oyly Carte production of *Patience*, the Gilbert and Sullivan operetta, had had its first performance at the Opéra Comique in London on 23 April 1881 and after six months had been transferred to the newly built Savoy Theatre where it continued to attract an enthusiastic audience for a further year. Blanche seems not to have been at the first night, for after breakfast the following morning Sullivan noted in his diary that he had driven to see her: 'still very weak and unwell'. She might not have enjoyed the libretto with its reference to 'A greenery yallery, Grosvenor Gallery . . . ' for she had no liking for the aesthetic move-ment – particularly if applied to the Grosvenor which was for the exhibition of art. How the public behaved there was irrelevant to its purpose, although she must have admitted it had added to its publicity.

A fortnight after the gallery's summer opening she was able to accompany Coutts to Florence for six weeks to see his mother. In August they were at Bad Homburg for her to take the cure; and here they had found Arthur Sullivan. As well as walking and dining with Coutts at the Kursaal, he had called several times on Blanche, finding her usually unwell. With her daughters she had spent 'the most sad autumn of 1881' in Munich and yet that very year she and Coutts had jointly written a song, 'Waft Me on a Wandering Dream',* music by Blanche, the words by Coutts, an unlikely combination for a couple soon to

* Appendix II

separate. In December Blanche was at Aston Clinton in a 'low and miserable state'; Constance was aware that she had some great trouble on her mind but felt unable to help her. Again with Constance in April the following year, she (Blanche) 'alas! was rather silly' at a lunch party which Louise Jopling had thrown over and at which Arthur Balfour was 'intensely fascinating'.

Coutts was in Rome that spring and in his diary Arthur Sullivan records having met him in William Wetmore Story's studio and later, having driven together to Acqua Paolo from which the view over the 'divine city' was magnificent, they drove home past Castel Sant' Angelo and had dined in Coutts's rooms at 72 Via Sistina.

Meanwhile Blanche had gone alone to Prince Leopold's wedding in St George's Chapel, Windsor, where arrayed in Court dress, feathers, diamonds and a long train she had found her seat next to the Dean of Christ Church (the prince's old college) and Mrs Liddell.

In Constance's view the 1882 Grosvenor Gallery exhibition was 'horrid and dull as ditch water'. It could have been no surprise to her when in September she received 'sad tidings' from Blanche who was most unhappy in her married life, nor when a few days later she appeared at Surrey House and, throwing herself upon a sofa, told her cousin her sad story.

No papers or family knowledge illuminate the precise reason for Blanche's departure with her children from Balcarres and her London home in November. The fundamental reason was most probably Coutts's refusal to relinquish Kate and his newly-named son, James Lindsay. There may have been other infidelities. Charles Hallé, who knew the couple well, observed that 'It was not to be expected that a high-spirited woman would accept a condition repugnant to her feelings in the interests of a picture-gallery, nor was Coutts prepared to make a sacrifice of his personal inclinations for a similar cause.'[60]

With Blanche's departure the brilliance with which she had invested the social spectacle at the Grosvenor Gallery and given it distinction was dimmed and never recaptured.

May Holford, 'broken down in mind and spirit', had called twice on Constance before the final rupture and had talked 'so nobly and so well' that Constance was moved to wonder how Blanche could have chosen her Bohemian friends when she might have had such a support as her sister-in-law. After a depressing and miserable interview with Coutts she had felt 'that wicked and unprincipled as his conduct has been, hers has been sadly at fault'; and from her husband, who had also seen Coutts, she had learned from his own account that his home life was a very sad one; nevertheless in some things she believed Blanche and could not believe him. 'Alas! Alas! what an ending to so bright a beginning, what a deterioration of character.' After the separation Blanche dropped the Lindsays and clung to the Rothschilds, too tight a grip perhaps for Constance's taste, who found her 'too egotistical talking of nothing but herself', and 'Blanche wore me out with her troubles'; and again: 'Blanche very trying she bores me, touches me, angers me.'

The younger generation of Lindsays had never learned the rights or wrongs of her quarrel with Coutts but there were no doubt faults on both sides. Coutts in his younger days 'must have given just cause for offence. She however was in her own way equally determined and the regime which did not start on the lines of assured happiness, ended in inevitable disaster.'

On leaving Cromwell Place Blanche moved immediately to a house in Onslow Square, No. 46, which she rented from the Misses Hanbury until in March 1883 Nos. 41 and 42 Hans Place were ready for occupation. Here she had joined two houses (as at Cromwell Place) and had turned the upper floor of No. 41 into a studio. Almost her first action that November had been to send Helen, just fourteen years old, to the Rothschild Banking House at New Court to implore help of her cousins in securing for her the rest of her dowry (a large sum had gone to the building of the Grosvenor Gallery) for fear that it might disappear with Coutts after the separation. Her own belongings from both houses, and anything she had bought, were scrupulously returned to her and it was probably this procedure that resulted in Blanche and Effie travelling to Colinsburgh that summer and signing a document prepared by a solicitor.

The ubiquitous Walburga Lady Paget, herself wintering in Rome, learning that Coutts had flown there to escape 'the intolerable boredom of his home', was surprised to find that after three months locked in W. W. Story's studio, all he had to show for it was a 'very hard picture lilac in tone of an entirely naked man, and a girl sitting near him mending a net. Nobody could imagine why the man had no clothes on.' She thought him a very peculiar man.[61]

30

Electricity and Discord

For some little time Coutts had shown interest in lighting the galleries with electricity and he now took the bold iniative of installing two small portable generating plants in an outbuilding behind the gallery. By so doing he was able to light his galleries with 'smokeless' electric light, a startling innovation.[62] This was in 1883; two years later there had been so many demands from neighbouring businesses in New Bond Street that he decided to build a much larger permanent generating station in the sub-basement of the gallery, which measured sixty-five feet long, twenty-one wide. At the same time he formed a company, 'Sir Coutts Lindsay and Co.'. Based on the Gaulard-Gibbs system, the generators appeared to be entirely satisfactory, producing a brilliant light with no noise, and it seemed probable that every light that Coutts could let would shortly be taken. The two large generators supplied alternating current at what for the time was an enormous electrical input (2,500 volts). The cables carrying the current operated from a tower on the gallery's roof and were then suspended from iron posts on rooftops. Although Coutts would write optimistically in November 1885 'that difficulties seem to melt away wonderfully', nevertheless there were troubles – the latest, in a 'fair way to being overcome', with the telephone company, whose wires were affected.

It had become evident by early 1886 that the system had run into technical difficulties and it was Ludovic Lord Crawford, having succeeded his father and Minnie's beloved husband in 1880 as 26th Earl of Crawford, who planned a complete reorganization. He appointed the young Sebastian de Ferranti, a brilliant twenty-one-year-old who had already won a reputation as an inventor of alternators and of other electrical equipment, as chief engineer. Drastic improvements went forward on a large scale in which heavy investment was required. Coutts, already financially embarrassed (the Grosvenor had never paid its way sufficiently), and his mother put up most of the money; Bob (recently created Lord Wantage) and Ludovic Crawford were joint shareholders. At this point mortgages at Balcarres had been called up and Coutts, quite unable to pay them off, found Bob disinclined to give him any assistance, having little faith in Coutts's grasp of business concerns. ('Coutts is very queer to deal with,' Ludovic Crawford told his wife, 'as he is as free as possible with his own money yet when he is to receive someone else's he is very hard and grasping.') 'You need not fear that I shall come to a break with Bob,' Coutts wrote to Anne, 'I am under the belief that he is acting as he supposes his duty but he is as cold as ice and as hard', adding, 'Everyone is as good as gold to me' – Coutts's charm had not deserted him.

He finally disclosed the news that he would be forced to sell Balcarres – 'it almost breaks my heart.' It must have saddened Anne deeply to see the house lost through her dear son's inability to understand money, his extravagance, and the intransigence of his married life. Negotiations between Lord Crawford, Coutts and Bob were effectively held up for some months by Blanche 'exacting her pound of flesh' with regard to her marriage settlement and certain securities, while at the same time asking a concession from Coutts enabling her to will her money to the girls at her death, thus passing over Coutts's enjoyment of the money for his life. Arrangements were made, finally enabling Coutts to divest himself of all business concerns with Blanche who would therefore have no more reason for 'raising H—l against him', as she had done lately, and Bob proved himself 'as firm a brother as an old Norseman could devise only now gold not steel are the weapons required in the broker'.

In the spring of 1886 Balcarres, so dear to the family, was bought by Lord Crawford, only a few steps removed in consanguinity, and ten years later Coutts, living in strict retirement in Roehampton, wrote feelingly to his cousin: 'I have no sons, the house is now yours not only through purchase but as nearest and dearest of kin, this gives me constant pleasure when I think of the old home.'

During these years the Grosvenor exhibitions continued to be successful. Burne-Jones triumphed with his *Wheel of Fortune* in 1883; in 1884 with *King Cophetua and the Beggar Maid*. Whistler had sent two canvases for that year, *Arrangement in Black: Lady Archibald Campbell*, and a portrait of Monsieur Theodore Duret, the art critic. This last Coutts had felt obliged to ask the artist to withdraw:[63] 'The work is so incomplete, so slightly made out I cannot accept it at the Grosvenor. I wish my dear Whistler that you would do yourself and me more justice and not send work that cannot do you or me credit.'

Portfolios of Old Master drawings from the Library of Christ Church, Oxford were made up at the subscription rate of five pounds, as well as an illustrated catalogue of the works by Reynolds which had formed the 1883-4 Winter Exhibition. The next year had seen a successful one-man show of Millais' works and an exhibition of Vandyck had yet to follow. The youthful Alfred Gilbert was exhibiting a statuette in 1886 when Coutts effected the introduction to Burne-Jones which was to have so great an influence on the direction of the sculptor's work.[64] 'Come along my boy, you must know my friend Burne-Jones . . . You are kindred spirits with methods and expression widely dissimilar.'[65]

In 1885 a 'Clergy Club' was created for clerics and lay members of the Church of England and of 'churches in communion therewith'; but it barely survived. The restaur-

ant had never defrayed its expenses. The 1885 Summer
Exhibition had 418 exhibits including Coutts's portrait of
Joseph Pyke, the Regent Street jeweller, a short-lived but
rather *louche* figure in the story of the Grosvenor, brought
in by Coutts to represent him as he was said to understand
Coutts's tangled affairs. (Violet Hunt declared that since
Blanche had taken away her money the Grosvenor was
'under obligation to Pyke, the Jew jeweller "Pyke of
Balcarres"'.[66]) Arthur Wade was another who came in with
Pyke, and Ludovic found his assistance useful when in the
summer of 1887 the London Electric Supply Corporation
was formed with twenty-eight major shareholders to back
de Ferranti's vision of an enterprise on so huge a scale that it
would eventually come to be called 'the forerunner of all the
great power stations of the kingdom'. The scheme was for a
new site at Deptford but with the Grosvenor Gallery
basement still operative, with 70 miles of cable capable of
supplying current for 30,000 lights. The area covered
extended from Regent's Park to the Thames and from the
Law Courts to Knightsbridge. Among the many in-
stallations supplied were seven theatres, fifteen clubs, eight
hotels and the Savoy Turkish baths, two churches, restaur-
ants, as well some of the great houses: those of the
Marquess of Salisbury and of Lord Wimborne in Arlington
Street, the Duke of Buckingham at Chandos House, the
Earls of Fife and of Crawford in Cavendish Square, Lord
Rosebery's in Berkeley Square, Marlborough House, that of
the Duke of Newcastle, and Cyril Flower's Surrey House.
Twice fire had stopped distribution to customers but the
gallery had been undamaged.

Coutts placed £50,000 in the new company. Of this his
brother, with courage, it was said, that might have earned
him a second V.C., invested a sum roughly equivalent
nowadays to £7m. Coutts left the responsibility of the
contracts in his cousin's hands to arrange the best possible
on behalf of the company and then, characteristically,

wanted to upset the agreements, referring all points to a lawyer who naturally enough would have felt himself obliged to give some opinion so as to gain his fee.

The next crisis and one that heralded the eventual demise of the Grosvenor Gallery was a collision between Hallé and Comyns Carr in opposition to Coutts in which Burne-Jones and other artists played a non-vocal but resolute part.[67]

In October 1887 Burne-Jones, the most peaceable of men, sent an apologetic communication to Hallé, troubled and anxious as he was, regarding the manner in which the Grosvenor was slipping from its original position where its name had been respected, to one where it was degraded and was fast losing caste. 'Clubs, feasts, concerts, parties, advertisements, placards and refreshments – how they all vex my soul!' He had spoken to no one about it but asked Hallé to hint to Coutts of his vexation as it was of serious importance to him and, he thought, he was not the only one to be apprehensive. Hallé and Carr, no doubt jealous of the Pyke/Wade influence, rose forcefully to the occasion. What Ludovic had first seen as 'a nice kettle of fish brewing' and then as a 'rumpus' was now translated into a 'Halli-carnassian split'.

Correspondence, contentious, verging on animosity, but always within the bounds of good manners, passed between the three protagonists. The complaints of Carr and Hallé written from the Beefsteak Club, the Arts Club, the Garrick Club, and the Avenue Studios, Fulham Road, were based on the vulgarity of the new conception of the gallery where almost every night during the season the rooms were let out for cheap dinners, teas, and oysters and other enter-tainments while certain artists claimed that their work was not precisely suitable for the decoration of a dining and dancing saloon. Even the employees were exasperated 'almost to mutiny'. The reputation of the gallery was crumbling and Coutts was attacked for allowing Messrs Pyke and Wade to maintain openly that they were the real masters, whereas they had allegedly been brought in on the strictly limited basis of controlling the finances so that the introduction of new blood might result in a profit for the gallery which was of no little importance to Coutts. If allowed to see the accounts, Carr and Hallé would challenge Pyke to prove that no profit had accrued. Without a word of explanation from Coutts they submitted without protest to the abrogation of an agreement which he himself had proposed to make them his partners. Their position had become untenable and it was impossible to endure any longer the personal indignity of being made responsible to the exhibiting artists for acts of folly and vulgarity which were degrading to the gallery; they felt they could no longer be party to principles of which they could not approve.

Coutts had immediately fixed a date for meeting and discussion and had failed to put in an appearance, but a few days later he wrote from his Talgarth Road studio – said to have been given him by Anne for the masterpieces he had in contemplation, though he had soon tired of the idea.[68] He had, and meant to keep, the entire control of the gallery in his own hands. Messrs Pyke and Wade had no voice in the matter beyond what he chose to give them but stubbornly refused to recognize that the artistic management of the Grosvenor should not lie with them, nor that the Pyke innovations would harm the gallery. Burne-Jones, hoping for reconciliation, weighed in with Hallé and Carr, optimistic that Coutts would yield for the common good. If this were not possible 'I for one should have to withdraw, with pain and reluctance – feeling miserable at the breakdown of so handsome an undertaking as it was.' To this letter no answer was received. On 31 October Hallé and Comyns Carr tendered their resignations of the appointments they had held as directors of the Grosvenor Gallery. These were accepted by Coutts, that never-failing charm compensating his friends with the assurance that he would come and see them in a day or two 'and in the meanwhile I remember only that we are old friends and brother artists'.

Coutts could hardly have realized to what misfortunes his stubbornness would lead him. Soon Pyke and Wade were scarcely on speaking terms; Wade was sacked and Coutts placed the management in the hands of a Captain Gordon, lately manager of the Langham Hotel, Portland Place, and appointed C. W. Deschamps, a young and most promising dealer, as his new temporary assistant. At the same time a 'Ladies restaurant par excellence' in the newly artistically decorated east gallery which looked onto New Bond Street was advertised as open for the supply of 'The Highest Class Luncheons and Dinners. The Choicest Wines only will be served. Mr B. G. Garibaldi, the Chef de Cuisine of the Grosvenor Gallery Restaurant Parisien will personally superintend.'

When, after the 1887 break-up, Burne-Jones informed Watts how sickened and discouraged he had been by the catastrophe which he had brought on himself and that he thought it was evident that the general public and press were on the side of Coutts, he was telling the truth. *The Artist*, *Punch*, the *Athenaeum*, *Vanity Fair* and others expressed their disapproval. *Vanity Fair* conceded that 'All the public care to know about the Grosvenor Gallery is that one can go in for 1/– if pictures are worth seeing. But whether Messrs Hallé and Carr are there or not we cannot care for we should certainly not pay 1/– to see either of them or both together.'[69] But in May 1888 these two successfully launched an exhibition at the hastily built New Gallery at the lower end of Regent Street with works by many of the artists whose paintings had enhanced the walls of the Grosvenor, including those of Burne-Jones, and this rival gallery would claim in future the greater names and the more brilliant successes.

For ten years the Grosvenor had held a pre-eminent

position of influence in the mounting of distinguished exhibitions in surroundings likened to an Italian palace. More importantly, it had offered an opening to younger painters, thus fulfilling a need for contemporary art. That it had been given an added impetus by the 'aesthetic movement' that had only increased its renown had evoked a certain hostility, but the conception of the gallery and its accountability were unique in its time and proved the introduction to a new epoch in the display of pictures.

Nothing if not optimistic, Coutts was in good heart though, as he said himself, 'Only remember I am fighting without much assistance.' There was the development of the Electric Supply Corporation which he could not neglect for a day. The building of the Central Station at Deptford was going ahead, a gigantic and successful task of constructing powerful machinery, engines and dynamos of unprecedented size.

Although he maintained in the autumn of 1888 that there was an improvement in the affairs of the gallery and was able to take a week's absence in the country on his tricycle, he was bound to admit that the New Gallery was a thorn in his side. 1889 saw the opening of a lending library offering a constant supply of new books in 'all classes of Literature, Foreign books, Music, Reviews and Magazines, as well as tickets for every Theatre and places of amusement'. This was not the way to save the Grosvenor and the Summer Exhibition of 1890 was its final one, leaving Coutts with the recollection of ten years of heady success and satisfaction and an overdraft of £111,000 at the bank.

The Final Departure

Blanche, meanwhile, outwardly at least, was having a rollicking good time. During her eighteen married years she had developed the necessary push to see her through what would then have been seen as the ambiguous position of a married name but no attendant husband, two adolescent daughters but no family home; but she had the world's opinion with her and she settled down to safeguard it.

Within a fortnight of installing herself in Onslow Square she had written to Robert Browning:

I think you must have heard by this time of all the sorrows that, after a long time, made me resolve not to live any more in my husband's house – I cannot write about them but I write a line to ask you to come and see me any day that you are in this direction. I have taken this little house for a little while for myself and my children.[70]

The Burne-Joneses had shown their sympathy by giving her the use of a studio next to Burne-Jones's own in the garden of The Grange and she would often stay to lunch; sometimes on Sundays she was invited to supper, to which only close friends were admitted. This was before the row at the Grosvenor Gallery and the sympathy may have been more on the part of Georgiana Burne-Jones who had a just perception of the mortification and pain of an erring husband.

The new year started briskly with Blanche enjoying a large dinner party given by Arthur Sullivan where Leighton and Alfred Rothschild were her old friends and after George Grossmith and his wife, assisted by Weedon Grossmith, had entertained the guests with a mock melodrama they sat down to supper and stayed till two in the morning. In March of this year Blanche moved to Hans Place and in the same month Gladstone's daughter saw her at Rossetti's posthumous exhibition at Burlington House: 'Poor deserted Lady Lindsay, a garish figure that almost destroyed sympathy.'[71] Her friendship with Louise Jopling had suffered an estrangement: in the past Blanche had appealed to her to see Coutts as much as possible when she was not at hand; this Louise had done but after the separation when Blanche had required of her to cut Coutts publicly she had refused to do so. The Rudolph Lehmanns were old and welcoming friends, and Lady Molesworth, still at her 'little dinners', celebrated the New Year of 1884 with a dinner for twenty-two and Blanche saw Lady Dorothy Nevill there among the large company. At the American Legation in Lowndes Square Henry James was one of the guests dining with James Russell Lowell, the American Minister. With Mrs John Hare, wife of the actor, Blanche was at the Savoy Theatre for the first night of *Princess Ida*.

At Millais' house at Palace Gate, Kensington, she saw Lord Houghton for the last time before his death, with Robert Browning the only other guest at dinner. She remembered the cold of the large studio on the first floor, herself in a fur coat and the firelight playing on Browning's white hair and beard. Lady Millais had withdrawn to another part of the house and had left them to it.

Aston Clinton had its quota of visits but there Blanche would abandon herself to her misery, which Constance would recognize but find very wearing. Froyle Park, Alton, the beautiful sixteenth-century house in Hampshire belonging to the thirty-six-year-old Sir Hubert Miller, Bt, was also a refuge, as was the church within the park where its patron was a lay reader. Blanche was much inclined towards religion and was known to have preferred to read the New Testament in Greek, and soon Effie, her eldest daughter, having on her mother's insistence been presented at Court, had departed to north London to train as a deaconess.

It was in July 1884 when preparing for a sojourn at Froyle that Blanche missed her footing on the very steep un-carpeted staircase leading down from her studio and fell headlong to a landing below, suffering contusion of the brain which left her an invalid for more than two years, with noise and light her worst enemies. Hans Place was being developed with all the accompanying clamour entailed, so, hoping to find quiet, Blanche and both daughters moved to a small countrified villa in St John's Wood. Here the house was kept in perpetual darkness, the windows covered with layers of black gauze and a lighted candle stub in a metal case the only illumination in Blanche's room. Helen looked after her mother faithfully for long, wearisome months and was called up at night when Blanche, who had slept throughout the day, would often show indications of cerebral activity and would dictate poetry to her daughter, who by the light of a flickering fire would transcribe the verse; or else in reading aloud would attempt a translation from the German of Grimm's *Fairy Tales*. Helen rarely left her mother's side, sometimes embroidering (when she could see to do it) a velvet binding for Blanche's book of Greek Gospels.

Once restored to health Blanche took up her life again at Hans Place. Glimpses of her evoked by Margaret's diaries[72] (the Burne-Joneses' daughter) give the impression of a perfect gadabout, calling at The Grange, going to the theatre with Burne-Jones, at a musical party in Alma-Tadema's studio amongst the Du Mauriers, Lady Airlie, Margot Tennant and others. Here she was described as 'with a girl', probably Helen, now twenty, who never left her mother until the latter's death nearly twenty-five years on – after which she went out as a missionary to China. It was known that 'Hardly anyone saw her [Blanche's] daughters especially when they had attained ages suggesting a maturing mother. They adored her and waited on her hand and foot and disliked their father with equal energy.' It is doubtful if they ever saw Coutts again after early November 1882.

Blanche had kept up her friendship with Princess Louise and in the summer of 1887, when entertaining the princess, she invited Watts, but as one whose day began at four in the morning and who was trying to complete his equestrian statue, *Physical Energy*, while the good weather lasted, he had no time to pay his respects.[73] That same summer Blanche's recollection of having seen Marie Vetsera, the suicide companion of Crown Prince Rudolph of Austria, at her cousin Ferdinand's house in Piccadilly a few months before the girl's death at Mayerling, was of a young woman in signal contrast to her mother beside whom she was seated. The elder woman, Baroness Hélène Vetsera, a Levantine, was all gesticulation, high complexion, bordering on vulgarity. Marie, not yet known to the prince, though she may well have seen him as he too was in London during the Queen's Jubilee celebrations, sat motionless and silent in a black gown, cut low, without jewels; her very dark hair was worn smooth and tightly braided close to her head; the eyes like dark velvet looked out from a face whose skin – and that of the neck and shoulders also – were whiter than Blanche had ever seen.

Although fairly sturdy in health now, a weakness in the eyes prevented her from painting so she turned her skills to writing. The rarefied atmosphere of 41 Hans Place where they were nine servants – lady's maids, parlour and housemaids, footman, butler, housekeeper and cook – to wait on Blanche and Helen, was best caught by a cousin of Coutts when describing how she lived 'in a stifling pictur-esqueness of tapestries, old embroideries and furniture and pictures – heavy hangings and airlessness'. It was in these rooms that Blanche 'received her devotees', from the world of artists, musicians and writers. As for the social world, it was only recently that she had dined with Constance at Surrey House where the guests included Alfred Lyttelton, Harry Cust and Rhoda Broughton, but it was in her own house that she led a ' "*Précieuses*" existence of choice *tête-à-têtes* and carefully flavoured personalities'. Here also was her beautiful and very tame yellow and green parrot which walked about, allowing her to tease or caress it.

On Ludovic Crawford's son, who had seen her only once, Blanche had left the impression of a 'great hulk of a woman with flamboyant gesture and the simulus of infantile grace'. She was clever and known as 'a *causeuse* of merit – but never overburdened with high principle or collective ambition'.

In early 1893 Cyril Flower was offered the Governorship of New South Wales which he was eager to accept but was prevented from doing so because his wife Constance could not bring herself to leave her mother, 'my dearest, most treasured possession'. Blanche busied herself with advice, writing to Constance, showing her how badly her conduct was perceived by others. Not content with one letter, she followed it up with another, pointing out to her cousin that she had shown Cyril that she thought of her mother first. 'I know I never got over leaving my mother as I did but then she was dying.'[74] (Blanche could not foresee that posterity would gauge the truth of that statement through her Aunt Charlotte's letters.) She thought Cyril's life had been hard with 'no interests or position at Aston Clinton and that he had behaved as not one man in a thousand would do'. These strictures upset Constance, for she realized their relevance and how she had 'blighted my dear Cyril's career and what years of misery we have before us'. He had earlier been created Lord Battersea and had bought himself a property, The Pleasaunce, at Overstrand, two miles from Cromer. This was his chief country home, in which he delighted, but Constance sighed into her diary that he still had plenty of time 'for endless complaints. *Never* satisfied with anything.'

Throughout these years Blanche's literary output was unremitting. Short stories followed a three-volume novel, *Bertha's Earl*; verses for children with her illustrations; a *Book of Robins*; carols and songs; a series of stories in *Aunt Judy's Magazine*. In *Caroline*, her first novel (1888), using one of her own names, the reader cannot avoid detecting autobiographical matter. Except for her quarterly issue of *Greenleaves*, poetry was her chief production. The small graceful books of poems, *The King's Last Vigil*, *The Flower Sellers*, *The Apostle of the Ardennes*, *The Prayer of St Scholastica*, *Love and Death*, were mostly presented in olive green cloth within bevelled boards, though the 1903 *From a Venetian Balcony* was on handmade paper, including pen sketches by Clara Montalba. This volume carried a poem 'In the Time of Lilies', a recognition of Mrs Eden's beautiful garden (called the Garden of Eden) at the Palazzo Barbarigo where she lived. But by now Blanche's visits to Venice had ceased. Robert Browning had told Constance that he had tried to persuade her to make the journey but on the whole he found her 'too complicated to travel'.

Besides these books of poetry there were quarterly leaflets issued under the title of *Greenleaves*, the first in April 1903. Bound in small, slim, square green covers, little gold embossed leaves framed the title. Each pamphlet was headed

'As of the green leaves on a thick tree, some fall, some grow.'
Ecclesiasticus, XIV, 18

and these, consisting of disjointed memories and verse were sent to friends.

One of Blanche's theories was that instead of celebrating birthdays 'we should look forward to our death-days', so perhaps it was with no common reluctance that she welcomed death on 4 August 1912 at Hans Place after a short illness of twenty-four hours.

In her will she left an annuity of £500 to the owner of Froyle where she had often spent the summer months; to the National Gallery she offered all the pictures in her drawing-room as a free gift.[75] Jewellery, furniture and plate were left to her daughters to divide and these were mostly sold at Christie's at the end of the year. They were also the beneficiaries of the residue of her estate; she singled out her portrait with the violin by G. F. Watts for Euphemia who had married the Reverend T. Selby Henrey, for many years vicar of St George's, Brentford. To Helen who had lived with her mother to the end and who would later marry George Ramsay, a Scot twenty years her junior, conscientious objector and the head of his own religious sect (but with few converts), Blanche had left letters, documents and private papers. These, destroyed by her descendants, included those letters restored after their mother's death: passionate letters Blanche had written to Coutts after the separation imploring him to come back to her, returned unread.

32
'I Feel More Cocky . . .'

With some few terse words written to his brother in March 1888 Bob conveyed the disapprobation of the Lindsays and friends of the way in which, to conceal his identity, Coutts had assumed a designation which in fact invited attention to his invidious position. Having disposed of Cromwell Place, Coutts was living at 52 Bedford Square with Kate and their son, calling himself 'Lt-Colonel Lindsay'. Bob objected that it would lead to embarrassment and complications. 'I allude to the scandal of the lady taking your name and her assuming the name of Lindsay.' He asked for an assurance that his name and address be altogether omitted in future directories. 'Lt-Colonel Lindsay' was still appearing as at Bedford Square in 1891[76] though by the beginning of the year he had installed Kate in a house in Roehampton Vale with James[77] their son, her mother Mrs Burfield, and Annie her younger sister. There were, besides, a housemaid and a cook. Kate Lindsay is given as 'married' and 'head' of the house in the 1891 public census and 'living on her own means'. Coutts's name does not appear, though perhaps he conveniently absented himself for the day. Once a stay-maker it is likely that Mrs Burfield, also 'living on her own means', was indebted to Coutts for this state of affairs. She had probably provided a home for Kate and James through the years, entirely or partly paid for by Coutts, and this may well have been one of Blanche's more serious accusations. James would shortly be serving with the Forfar and Kincardine Artillery and would marry in a few years; Annie, the sister, married and departed, and Mrs Burfield would have been settled elsewhere.

The house, Roehampton Villa, the first on the north side of the Vale but set well back, was of a fair size with an extensive garden containing a mulberry tree as well as a walled fruit garden. Next came a pillar box, then a few cottages in one of which, Vine Cottage, Ellen Terry lived in 1903. These were the only contestants for this secluded piece of countryside which for two centuries had been the 'aristocratic part of Putney'. The windows on the back looked through tall chestnuts onto Richmond Park while in front, though at some little distance, lay the grassy acres and quiet serenity of Putney Cemetery, opened in 1891, where once had been orchards and open fields.

This retirement, under the name of 'Colonel Coutts Lindsay' was what he wished for and in later years he would say that it was for Kate he had sacrificed his title and his career. In the irregularity of this relationship even Coutts had jibbed at giving her the appellation of 'Lady Lindsay' (with Blanche still in the wings to ferment trouble). His career had been a life given to the practice of art but with society biased gainst him and with the end of the Grosvenor and in particular the successful opening of the New Gallery, he preferred to withdraw altogether. He would visit only the most intimate members of his family and receive even fewer. His sister May had died in 1892, his mother in 1894. She had lived chiefly at Ardington House, close by Lockinge, with frequent visits to her children and grandchildren – with the exception of Coutts, whom she had loved with 'ineradicable tenaciousness of heart' while recognizing his imperfections. Though it cost her much pain, 'she remained steady in declining to visit his Roehampton settlement, although repeatedly urged to do so'.

His brother, younger than Coutts by ten years, had died in 1901 though not before he and his wife had again come to Coutts's financial assistance. Minnie died in 1909. But apart from lumbago, which he was hoping to cure with massage and Turkish baths, Coutts was well enough to go on a country expedition with Kate in a dog-cart. From 'High Wickham' they had made a pilgrimage to Hughenden where a child's burial was taking place not far from Lord Beaconsfield's tomb. With horse and trap they had driven on through 'pastoral country' in August sunshine with Matlock and Buxton as their goal. But the years were beginning to tell. Coutts had been seriously ill in early 1912 but his conversation was still stimulating and full of force, his criticism on artistic subjects always original. Slow and old-fashioned in his diction, he could draw from a long and almost inexhaustible experience of men and things. 'Poor gallant old fellow, it is sad how his life has been discounted,' observed a relation. 'His was a wasted life. Too versatile, too fond of experiment, he never allowed himself to master the theory of work, too impatient ever to get beyond the ambit of the dilettante and amateur.'

Now his chief anxiety was for Kate, who had cared for him 'with singular love and fidelity'; how beneficial it would be 'if Blanche who has now reached a ripe old age [sixty-eight years] could be peacefully borne to the bosom of Abraham and that the last few years or months of his life might be decorously redeemed from an irregular marriage *de la main gauche*.' These hopes would find fulfilment within six months. With Blanche dead, would Coutts marry Kate?

With utmost haste and within six days of his first wife's death Coutts and Kate were married in the Wandsworth Register Office, Coutts giving his age as eighty-six[78] and Kate, aged sixty-two, as the widow Madley. Their son James, Kate's sister, and a Lindsay cousin were witnesses. This last reported that Coutts was very nervous at the ceremony but that '*she* was and is overbubbling with joy'.

The next step was for Coutts to make his will. Everything was to go to Kate but in the event of her dying before him, then 'Arthur Harris Burfield Madley (commonly known as James Lindsay)' was to inherit his father's estate, allowing three hundred pounds a year to Annie and to Mrs Burfield. The witnesses to his will were the gardener and the chauffeur – a motor car had now replaced the pony-cart. To this a codocil had been added with instructions that such securities as were thought fit should be set apart to produce one hundred pounds per annum and this income to be paid to Coutts Lindsay Chambers during his life 'or until he shall become bankrupt'.

In J. M. Jopling's drawing of Coutts standing outside the Grosvenor Gallery he is seen wearing a hat the design of which was peculiar to the Lindsays; when early in 1913 a cousin of a younger generation called on him it seemed that the brim 'had assumed a more sweeping curve – upwards'. He rallied its wearer 'on the rakish novelty of the hat. "I wonder if that is really so", Coutts replied, "but in any case it may well be for I feel more cocky than I have done for many years past."'

Since his marriage 'a fresh zeal had come into his life, a blitheness of touch and outlook most remarkable in a man of eighty-nine'. But his health, though unimpaired, was frail; gallstones were his enemy. His heart failed him and he died on 7 May 1913. Born in the reign of George IV he had lived to see George V come to the throne and had departed a year before the Great War.

The funeral service was held at Kingston Vale, the interment in the churchyard of St Andrew's, Ham. There Coutts lies under a large inscribed cross and beneath the wide sweep of the sky.

The chief mourners, so The Times of 14 May reported, were the Earl of Crawford, James Lindsay (now a lieutenant-colonel) and May Holford's son, Colonel Sir George Holford. The following day in the Court Circular column of The Times, the newspaper announced that they had been requested to state that Lady Lindsay, the second wife of Sir Coutts Lindsay, had been present as chief mourner both at the service and at the interment.[79]

It is not possible to form an opinion of the artist's performance as so few examples appear to have survived, whether through the vagaries of fashion, the ravages of war, or else the deficiencies of the works themselves. Perhaps in clearing out Balcarres at the time of his departure Coutts destroyed what surely amounted to dozens upon dozens of sketches, while Kate, who survived him until 1937, may have disposed of many of the paintings. It is disappointing that a man with such a lifelong devotion to works of art in many forms should have left little trace of his own endeavours.

There had existed a warmth and understanding between the eighty-nine-year-old Coutts and his very much younger cousin, now 27th Earl of Crawford, grandson of Minnie and Lord Lindsay, Coutts's early and loved mentor. Of Coutts he wrote:

As a soldier, landlord, artist and man of business he was alternately distinguished and enterprising, always original and interesting yet his labours were never crowned with success. Lack of patience and stedfastness marked his career throughout, except in the ceaseless and unchanging devotion he lavished on Kate. Nevertheless with all his faults he was one of the most attractive personalities I ever met. I shall never forget his dignity and charm – they outbalanced all his human shortcomings. He was a good man who assuredly ought to have been a great one.

Lady Bank Station
17th Sept. 2–3 o'clock
1874

Dear Lady Lindsay just one line to say
How much my wife & I enjoyed our stay
And of our grateful thoughts how great a share is
Due to our charming hostess at Balcarres.
The noises in this God-forsaken station
Are 'base accompaniment' to inspiration.
But, fresh from you, my mind is so aesthetic
That, even here, I'm forced to be poetic.
Melons & models, melodies & mirth
Still float before us on our way to Perth,
Yet scarce I dare to sing in doggerel rhyme
The bright impression of that handsome time.
Fitly to sing its glories, I'd require
To drink of Sullivan's melodious fire.
Truly to paint its warm & sunny flush
I'd need the colours of fair Jopling's brush.
How shall I tell the zest with which we fell on
The luxurious lumps of the nine pounder melon?
What rounded compliments, what pretty speeches
Would do full justice to our feasts of peaches?
Yet hush! how ill these greedy thoughts become
Guests who have basked in your aesthetic home,
So steeped in art, that even every rose
Seems bent on blooming in a perfect pose.
Full many a day my mem'ry will recall
The panelled chamber and the armoured hall!
The gems of art, the dazzling shell of roses
In which each day we bathed our happy noses.
Still in my thoughts, I see your happy look

Glancing so bright above your music book,
While o'er the keys your gentle fingers stray
And waft around us Schubert's sweetest lay.
Yet there are moments when the mood in favour
Was somewhat spiced with a Bohemian flavour,
And when o'er fruit and wine in merry session
We each in turn made terrible confession.
But hark! the distant locomotive's whistle
Warns me 'tis time to finish this epistle.
And so goodbye! I've only still to say,
I hope, 'the patient victim' sat to-day
And that in spite of dressing & undressing
The painter's work is rapidly progressing.
How clear before me still your figure gleams
Your eyes brimful of some delicious dreams,
A model lovely model – but alack!
The parts are changed: 'tis *I* am 'looking back'.[80]

GEORGE GOSCHEN

The answer

Balcarres,
Colinsburgh,
September 20th 1874   Fife.

How can a woman, not at all poetical,
Reply to one so talented as you?
I can but pray you, do not be too critical,
For if my verse be poor, my words are few.
How shall I thank you for the happy notion
Which turned your thoughts into such graceful rhyme,
And caused you to indite, dear Mr Goschen,
Your lovely record of 'our lovely time'?
Each of our guests in turn has praised it duly,
Our minds are filled with a respectful awe;
For who but an enlightened statesman, truly,
Could from rude 'Lady bank' his thoughts withdraw,
And bend his mind back to its usual functions,
With ministerial tact ignore
Our ghastly Caledonian junctions,
And to the realms of verse & music soar.

If such the rule of statesmen & of radicals,
If, merman-like, they charm us with their song,
Then let us joyfully put on our manacles,
And bind ourselves with red tape, sure & strong;
And praise the sound & liberal education
Which gave you over time & tide such power,
You could forget, not your, but our poor station,
And make the most of such a short lived hour!
Do not forget the circle that you brightened
With happy jests and words of ready wit,
Which, as you spoke, the bonds of friendship tightened,
And all our hearts in pleasant converse knit.
We all regret you – if you wish to please us,
Return to this our friendly northern land,
Return to chaff & chafe, & charm & teaze us,
And feel the 'warm grasp' of my cordial hand!
My husband bids me add, with much emotion,
How willingly he would your steps beguile,
Ah, that Balcarres were your 'land of Goschen',
You & your wife would tarry here awhile!

APPENDIX II

Waft Me on a Wandering Dream

Waft me on a wandering dream
That my soul may float away
On the fancy's vagrant stream
Soft rock'd till day.
Float me, float me, float me, float me,
Soft rock'd till day.

Strand me on thy loving breast
There I fain would beat and lie.
Thy poor mariner at rest
Where I would die.
Strand me, strand me, strand me, strand me,
Where I would die.

Select Bibliography

All books are published in London unless otherwise stated

Adam, E., *Mrs J. Comyns Carr's Reminiscences*, 1926.

Apollo Magazine, June 1964; November 1975.

Balfour, E., *Magazine of Art*, 1883.

Barker, Nicolas, *Bibliotheca Lindesiana*, Roxburghe Club, 1977.

Battersea, Constance, *Reminiscences*, 1922.

Benson, E.F., *Final Edition*, 1940.

Blunt, Wilfrid, '*England's Michelangelo*', 1955.

Builder, The, 1877.

Bullen, Dr Barrie, 'The Palace of Art', *Apollo Magazine*, November 1975.

Burne-Jones (G.B-J), *Memorials of Edward Burne-Jones*, ii, 1904.

Carr, J. Comyns, *Some Eminent Victorians*, 1908.

Carr, Mrs J. Comyns, *Stray Memories*, 1920.

Cecil, Lord David, *Visionary & Dreamer*, 1969.

Chancellor, E. Beresford, *The Private Palaces of London Past*, 1908.

Cochrane, Rob, *Pioneers of Power*, 1987.

Colvin, Sydney, ed., and compiled by Lionel Cust, *History of the Dilettanti*, 1898.

Cook, E.T., and Alexander Wedderburn, edd., *The Works of John Ruskin*, XVIII, 1903–1912.

Country Life, 1928.

Dorment, Richard, *Alfred Gilbert*, Yale University Press for the Mellon Centre for Studies in British Art, 1985.

Fife News, September 1877.

Fitzgerald, Penelope, *Edward Burne-Jones*, 1975.

Fraser's Magazine, June 1862.

Gifford, M.J., ed., *Pages from the Diary of an Oxford Lady*, Shakespeare Head Press, Oxford, 1932.

Gosse, Edmund, *Father and Son*, 1907.

Hallé, C.E., *Notes from a Painter's Life*, 1909.

Harbron, Dudley, *The Conscious stone*, 1949.

Hare, Augustus, *The Story of Two Noble Lives*, 1893.

Hare, Augustus, *The Story of My Life*, v, 1900.

Hayman, John, ed., *John Ruskin, Letters from the Continent*, University of Toronto Press, 1982.

Henrey, Robert, *A Century Between*, 1937.

Hicks, Seymour, *Between Ourselves*, 1930.

Hillier, Bevis, 'The St John's Wood Clique', *Apollo Magazine*, June 1964.

Hussey, Christopher, *Country Life*, LXIII, 1928.

Illustrated London News, The, 1877, 1887.

Jacobs, Arthur, *Sir Arthur Sullivan*, O.U.P., 1984.

Jopling, Louise, *Twenty Years of My Life*, 1925.

Laver, James, *Whistler*, 1930.

McAllistar, Isabel, *Alfred Gilbert*, 1929.

Magazine of Art, 1883.

Masterman, Lucy, ed., *Mary Gladstone*, 1930.

Matheson, Glenis, and Taylor, Frank, *Handlist of Personal Papers from the Muniments of the Earl of Crawford and Balcarres*, The John Rylands, University of Manchester, 1976.

Ormond, Leonée, *George Du Maurier*, 1969.

Paget, Walburga Lady, *Embassies of Other Days*, ii. 1923.

Paget, Walburga Lady, *Linings of Life*, ii, 1928.

Portfolio, The, 1877.

Punch, 1873–82.

Ritchie, Hester, ed., *Letters of Anne Thackeray Ritchie*, 1924.

Rooke, T.M., 'Notes of Conversations of E. Burne-Jones', Victoria and Albert Museum typescript, IV.

Ross, Janet, *The Fourth Generation*, 1912.

Sala, Augustus, *The Life and Adventures of G.A. Sala*, 1895.

Steegman, John, *Consort of Taste*, 1950.

Stroud, Dorothy, *Humphry Repton*, 1962.

Survey of London, (Mayfair), XL, iii.

Towndrow, K.R., *Alfred Stevens*, 1939.

Vanity Fair, 1887.

Wantage, H., *Lord Wantage, V.C., K.C.B., A Memoir*, 1907.

Source Notes

1 The 22nd Earl of Crawford had died leaving no male kin. Alexander 6th Earl of Balcarres was *de jure* the 23rd Earl but the title had remained in abeyance until 1848 when Lord Lindsay had been successful in claiming the earldom of Crawford for his father (the son of Alexander), for till then he had been known as 7th Earl of Balcarres.

2 Repton's 'Red Books' contained reports on his landscape proposals together with a series of sketches and overslips, bound up in red.

3 If Angela Burdett did not survive or was childless or married a foreigner (which eventually she did), the estate was to pass to her sister and if herself childless it was to go to a third sister. In the event of all three sisters dying without children a portion of the inheritance was to go to Coutts Lindsay. Angela Burdett, on inheriting from the Duchess of St Albans, added 'Coutts' to her name.

4 Lord David Cecil, *Visionary & Dreamer*, 80.

5 Edmund Gosse, *Father and Son*.

6 Rev Henry Blunt, *Exposition of the Pentateuch*, 3 volumes. 'For family reading; Evangelical, practical, and earnest piety and beauty of language.'

7 'Molesworth, as spendid as a pea-hen on a sunny day.' *Letters to Anne Thackeray Ritchie*, 80.

8 Mr Mackenzie cannot be identified. John Delane was the celebrated editor of *The Times* for thirty-six years, 1841–77.

9 Balloon parties and races were greatly in fashion that summer. For instance, at Cremorne Gardens in August the Green brothers, well-known aeronauts, directed an aerial race to Wimbledon.

10 Walburga Lady Paget, *Linings of Life*, ii. 362.

11 John Steegman, *Consort of Taste*, 273.

12 The younger daughter, Lady Constance Leveson Gower, married Hugh Lupus, 1st Duke of Westminster.

13 The 2nd Earl had died in 1852 when Lord Eastnor succeeded to the title as 3rd Earl. Violet Hunt's Diaries, from which

passages are taken, are at Cornell University.

14 Caroline Norton's letter was characteristically enthusiastic. 'I think it is *magnificent*. It has the stir in it of that wild picture of war by Rubens that used to hang in the poet Roger's dining room. It is marvellous to me how any one in these tame, mechanised over-civilized days could so vividly recreate what I doubt not *was* the world, half animal nature of the poor Britons and their savage Queen, savage in the simpler sense of fierceness.' The 'wild picture of War' was Rubens's study for his *Terrors of War* (Pitti Palace, Florence).

15 ed. John Hayman, John Ruskin: *Letters from the Continent*, 37, 39.

16 An unfinished study by Watts of Coutts's head, made perhaps for this large design, survived until fairly recently. Its present whereabouts are not known though a photograph exists at the Watts Gallery.

17 ed. M. J. Gifford, *Pages from the Diary of an Oxford Lady*, 107. Augustus Hare thought the gardens would be beautiful 'if they were not spoilt by too many pine and araucarias and the house, a hideous castle of Otranto, occupying a noble situation.' A. Hare, *The Story of My Life*, v. 222.

18 Passages from letters and diaries of Constance de Rothschild (Lady Battersea) are quoted from the Battersea Papers, British Library.

19 Information derived from the Society of Antiquaries and from *History of the Dilettanti*.

20 Steegman, 185; Janet Ross, *The Fourth Generation*, 24.

21 In 1859 Bulwer-Lytton had published *The Haunted and the Haunters*.

22 Information derived from E. Balfour, *Magazine of Art*, VI, 1883; E. Beresford Chancellor, *The Private Palaces of London Past*, 1908; Christopher Hussey, *Country Life*, LXIII, 1928; K. R. Towndrow, *Alfred Stevens*, 1939. Letter from R. H. Benson to D. S. MacColl, Victoria and Albert Museum. The great sideboard from the dining-room and a set of eight mirrors in parcel-gilt walnut frames are in the Walker Art Gallery, Liverpool. The chimney-piece for the same room is in the Victoria and Albert Museum (Gamble room).

23 Paget, *Embassies of Other Days*, ii, 300.

24 Hare, *The Story of Two Noble Lives*, iii, 245.

25 Wife of the 7th Duke, she was the daughter of the 3rd Marquess of Londonderry and a dominating figure. It is questionable whether Blanche would have fared any better than she did in her own marriage. Lord Blandford married the

daughter of the 1st Duke of Abercorn in 1869 and was divorced in 1883 having eloped in 1881 with the Countess of Aylesford who, it was said, had borne him a son in 1882. This had provoked a notorious *cause célèbre*.

26 All passages from Baroness de Rothschild's letters are quoted from the Rothschild Archive. Marks of omission have not been introduced.

27 This was the London house of the Mentmore Rothschilds. The Lionel de Rothschilds lived at 148 Piccadilly.

28 'Natty', Baron Nathaniel de Rothschild, that is to say Hannah FitzRoy's brother and the only member of her family to have supported her at her wedding, was married to Charlotte, daughter of Baron James de Rothschild (of Ferrières) and should not be confused with Baron Lionel de Rothschild's wife, the chronicler of these present events. 'Alfy' (Alfred), referred to on 9 June, is the latter's son and remained a bachelor.

29 A slip for Princes Gate where the Somerses now lived at No. 33.

30 Perhaps Titian's portrait, *Eleonora Gonzago, Duchess of Urbino* (Uffizi Gallery, Florence).

31 A blue plaque on the outside of No. 5 commemorates the artist, Sir John Lavery, who lived there 1899–1940.

32 With his death in 1917 the property was sold. Gunnersbury Park is now a local history museum.

33 Ferdinand de Rothschild, who built Waddesdon Park, was the widower of Evelina.

34 D. Wilkie Wynfield, painter and photographer, was the founder of St John's Wood Clique, a colony of artists who exhibited regularly at the Royal Academy, their portrayals of historical scenes and romantic incidents marking them out for success. For their own entertainment and to escape into the past they dressed up in costume. Bevis Hillier, 'The St John's Wood Clique', *Apollo*, June 1964. Coutts was not a member but would occasionally join in their amusements buckling on his armour of which he had a fine collection.

35 Helen Lindsay repeated what her mother had told her: that at the time this portrait was made there was a young woman staying in the house, a guest of Coutts, with whom he was in love and who was in the room while he was painting his wife. Unwilling to look at her, Blanche turned away her head. This is unlikely; the head in profile constitutes a charming composition which no doubt was what was projected. R. Henrey, *A Century Between*, repr. facing 184.

36 J. Comyns Carr, *Some Eminent Victorians*, 119–20.
37 L. Jopling, *Twenty Years of My life*, 74.
38 A. Jacobs, *Arthur Sullivan*, 82.
39 The Pierpont Morgan Library, New York.
40 Ibid; also *Arthur Sullivan* as above, 97.
41 Jopling, 92–3.
42 Letter in the National Portrait Archives. At the time of his death Coutts was the senior Trustee.
43 Information derived principally from the following sources: *The Builder*, XXXV, 1877; B. Bullen, 'The Palace of Art', *Apollo*, November 1975; G.B-J., *Memorials of Edward Burne-Jones*, ii, 69, 77–9; C.E. Hallé, *Notes from a Painter's Life*, 99; D. Harbron, *The Conscious Stone*, 123–4; R. Henrey, *A Century Between*, 198–205; *The Illustrated London News*, 9, 19 May 1877; L. Jopling, *Twenty Years of My life*, 114, 115; *The Portfolio*, 1877; *Survey of London*, XL, iii.
44 A photograph taken before the destruction of Santa Lucia proves that wherever the portal came from, it was not from that church. Its possible origin may have been the Palladian doorway of the Scuola Grande di Santa Maria della Misericordia before it too was destroyed. After 1864 much was sold and dispersed. A contemporary photograph of the Scuola Grande shows that the door was not unsimilar to that of the Grosvenor Gallery. For this information I thank Mr J. G. Links.
45 L. Ormond, *George Du Maurier*, 1969; *Punch*, 1873–82.
46 During the playing of *The Grasshopper*, a burlesque from the French *La Cigale*, which opened at the Gaiety Theatre on 8 December 1877, a mock Whistler landscape was brought onto the stage as representing 'A Desert Scene'; when reversed 'A Sunset at Sea'. D. Harbron, *The Conscious Stone*, 124.
47 edd. E. T. Cook and A. Wedderburn, *The Works of John Ruskin, Fors Clavigera*, Letter 79, July 1877, 157–8, 160.
48 This and the following extracts from Lord Henry Somerset's letters are quoted from private papers at Eastnor Castle.
49 G. A. Sala, *The Life and Adventures of G. A. Sala*, ii. 377.
50 ed. E. Adam, *Mrs Comyns Carr's Reminiscences*, 43, 57–8.
51 Much of this account is taken from the *Fife News*, Pierpont Morgan Library.
52 Mrs Carr's *Reminiscences*, 241.

53 Information given me by the Curator, Pierpont Morgan Library.

54 Seymour Hicks, *Between Ourselves*, 54.

55 Hallé, 113.

56 E. F. Benson, *Final Edition*, 50.

57 Jopling, 164.

58 'For her feet have touch'd the meadows/And left the daisies rosy.' *Maud*, i, xii, 6. In *Sesame and Lilies* 'Ruskin treats the passage as "a lover's fancy, false and vain!", as an instance that is, of the "Pathetic Fallacy". The poet resented this interpretation.' *Works of John Ruskin*, XVIII, 141–2 and *n*.

59 Jopling, 174–6.

60 Hallé, 152–3.

61 Paget, *Linings of Life*, ii. 338. Violet Hunt wrote of an Italian model he had run away with to Italy.

62 Information derived from R. Cochrane, *Pioneers of Power*; N. Barker, *Bibliotheca Lindesiana*, 296; ed. F.H.W. Sheppard, *Survey of London*, XL, iii.

63 Glasgow University Library. It was not until 1892 that the title of the painting was modified to *Arrangement in Black; Lady in the Yellow Buskin, Lady Archibald Campbell*, when attention was drawn to the yellow boot.

64 R. Dorment, *Alfred Gilbert*, 60.

65 I. McAllistar, *Alfred Gilbert*, 145.

66 V. Hunt, Diaries.

67 Information derived from *Printed Correspondence with Sir Coutts Lindsay*. Castle Howard archives.

68 T. M. Rooke, 'Notes of Conversation among the P.R. Brotherhood', IV. Typescript copy, Victoria and Albert Museum.

69 *Vanity Fair*, XXXVIII, 5 November, 1887, 297.

70 22 November 1882. The Beinecke Rare Book and Manuscript Library, Yale University.

71 ed. Lucy Masterman, *Mary Gladstone*, 283.

72 Information derived from diaries in private ownership.

73 Letter in the Huntington Library, San Marino, California.

74 This passage from Blanche's letter is quoted from the Battersea Papers.

75 These were accepted but have now been reassigned to studio work or imitators, with the exception of Ghirlandaio's *SS Justus and Clement of Volterra*.

76 According to directories for 1891 Coutts was living at Bedford Square but this does not correspond with the public census for that year in which his name does not appear.

77 In the 1891 public census James is listed without a surname.
78 He was eighty-eight. Perhaps Coutts had never divulged his correct age to Kate.
79 Kate Lindsay survived until 1937 and is buried in the grave at Ham with her husband.
80 In the possession of John Lindsay Jopling.

Index